Laughing Pilgrims

Humor and the Spiritual Journey

Howard R. Macy

Paternoster:
thinking faith

Cover Design by Design by James Kessell for Scratch the Sky Ltd
(www.scratchthesky.com)
Typeset by Westkey Ltd., Falmouth, Cornwall
Print Management by Adare Carwin
Manufactured in the United States of America.

For
Mahlon and Hazel,
my parents,
who made humor at home

and Nathan and Hannah,
my children
and dearest captive audience,
who laughed, groaned,
and stared uneasily

Table of Contents

Foreword

Richard J. Foster

I must begin by telling you that Howard Macy is a good friend of mine … a very good friend. And along with his impressive scholarship and gravitas I have to say that he is a funny person … a very funny person. Now, because Howard is my friend I am trying hard to guard against praising this book too much. But, in honesty, I must say that this is a funny book … a very funny book.

I am glad Howard Macy has turned his attention to humor and the spiritual journey. Modern stereotypes of religious folk as grim-faced killjoys abound. And there is enough truth in the stereotype for it to sting. Truth be told, Christian discipleship is serious business and it is something of an occupational hazard for those who take their discipleship seriously to become nothing more than serious. But serious lives need joy to maintain perspective. Besides, exuberant joy is the hallmark of the saints of old. Think of Francis, that little monk of Assisi, the troubadour of the Lord inebriated with the love of God – now that is a good model for us of a joyous spirituality. And, after all, God is the most joy-filled, completely happy being in the universe. So laughter and fun and good humor are all part of a vital, well-seasoned spirituality.

One reason this book is so much fun – and it truly is fun – is the skill Macy has as a wordsmith. *Laughing Pilgrims* is simply a joy to read. I found myself constantly delighting in the clever word choices. No one else I know would think to speak of our "klutz chromosome" or of the "vendors of grim" or to set up a recorded telephone message which says, "Incontinence Hotline. Can you please hold?"

But *Laughing Pilgrims* is a lot more than one-line zingers. It is thoughtful in ways that do not detract from its humor but indeed enhance the humor and make it all the more enjoyable. I'm sure you, like me, have seen stand-up comics who from all appearances have not given a single serious thought to the issue of humor ... likely no thought of any kind. For them getting a laugh is all that counts, no matter how cutting or self-serving or injurious or degrading the remark. To be sure, humor of any kind is risky, for when we use its techniques of pushing boundaries or saying the unexpected or exaggerating we, as Macy puts it, "tip-toe near the edge of a cliff." And sometimes we inadvertently slip over that edge. But inadvertently slipping is one thing; utter disregard for the cliff and all those we push over it with coarse, unthinking humor is quite another.

Here is where *Laughing Pilgrims* is such a help. And it is a help without stifling the fun. The chapter on "Sneaky Truth, Sneaky Lies" is particularly good here. Macy cleverly shows us how humor can sometimes function in the service of truth by catching us off-guard, by showing incongruity and absurdity, by surprise and exaggeration. Humor can also cloud truth at times in order to soften it. It's a way of marking boundaries, of showing courtesy and kindness. But we all know the ways humor can also be used to betray truth: deceiving us, hoodwinking us, assaulting us, destroying us.

For me the finest line in *Laughing Pilgrims* is Macy's challenge, "What would happen if our humor were to grow out of our dearest values?" Taking up such a challenge might well help us laugh with others more than at them. It might even promote a humor of generous compassion. Would it produce a greater wholeness in us? I wonder. My guess is that it most certainly would help us have far more joy in our humor without the acid aftertaste.

I greatly appreciate Chapter 6, "When It's Hard to Laugh." It is a difficult chapter to include in a book dedicated to humor, but I am glad for its inclusion. Happily I can report that it succeeds in dealing with a tough topic in both a respectful and humorous way. When speaking of the ravages of cancer Macy writes, "I saw a woman who was completely bald sporting a shirt that read 'Hair by Chemo.' Her demeanor showed joy and courage without denying the seriousness of her challenge." When talking with us about the losses that come with aging he writes, "We may repeat ourselves or struggle with memory or repeat ourselves." Earlier in the book Macy reminds us that "If the sky really is falling, humor may … serve as a hard hat to help us through." And so it does.

I'm glad for *Laughing Pilgrims*. I commend it to you.

Richard J. Foster
Christmas Eve, 2005

Preface

This book sneaked up on me. I had set out to suggest some principles for identifying and interpreting humor in the Bible, since books on biblical interpretation routinely neglect this. Though I knew my colleagues struggled to take me seriously when I told them I was working on humor, I simply hoped it would help people read the Bible. What I was learning about humor and Scripture, however, soon took surprising directions. It intersected with important themes in spiritual formation.

No doubt you know that most writing on spiritual growth forgets to include good laugh-out-loud humor. We're serious about this, you know. But I began to see that humor actually has a lot to do with how we understand ourselves, how we see the world, how we relate effectively with others, and, ultimately, how we come to glad wholeness in our lives. So I want to share what I've discovered about how humor can be a practical measure and tool in the spiritual journey.

Humor is a shared experience. We enjoy laughing together and making each other laugh. Because I hope you will enjoy doing that around the themes of this book, we have included questions to prompt reflection and response. You may enjoy them alone, of course, but you'll have even more fun sharing them with others. We're also going to experiment with a website, www.laughingpilgrims.com, as a place where readers can share ideas, responses, resources, and stories with one another. Maybe you'll join us there.

I am grateful for all those who encouraged and taught me in the process of writing this book. Special thanks go to my wife, Margi, and my adult children, Nate and Hannah, who wanted to share their pain. Thanks also to a circle of dear friends and to my great colleagues in Religious Studies at George Fox University, all of whom thought my doing this was amusing. My students at George Fox University have generally been kind as I've tried out new ideas. Two other groups of students have been especially helpful in testing these insights, one at the Center for Christian Studies in Reedwood Friends Church (Portland, Oregon) and the other at Pendle Hill, a Quaker study center in Wallingford, Pennsylvania.

Several friends have read the manuscript carefully and made valuable suggestions. If they weren't such fine persons I would be happy to blame them for any remaining flaws. University colleagues Paul Anderson, Irv Brendlinger, Mark McLeod-Harrison, and Arthur Roberts gave helpful counsel. Don Schroeder, a Presbyterian pastor who still chuckles at how slow I was to catch on to the idea of "lectionary," gave generous and cheerful help. I am deeply indebted to Tom Mullen, who knows humor and writing so well. He was especially generous with his laughter, Zinnserian wisdom, and hospitality. He even took me to Little Sheba's Sandwich Shop in Richmond, Indiana – a hot spot for folks in the know, with great sandwiches and servers who see the body as a canvas for tattoo art. I almost worry that I embarrassed him there, but I'll always cherish his friendship. Our department's administrative assistant, Margaret Fuller, has been wonderful in supporting this work along with work-study assistants Sarah Angell, Josh Kaiser, and Patrick Willis.

I am convinced that God intends us all to live in great joy and freedom, and I'll grin and giggle whenever God uses this book to help bring readers more fully into that life. Joy and blessings!

Howard Macy
December 2005

Part I
Discovering Ourselves
through Laughter

1

Humor Alert

Let's talk about laughing. Better yet, let's talk about laughter and the spiritual journey. Right away that sounds odd, I know, like an oxymoron: jumbo shrimp, affordable health insurance, laughing spirituality. Perhaps it would help to remember that the spiritual journey has to do with all of life, not just with consecrated chunks set off in a corner. So if Brother Lawrence could experience God fully while peeling potatoes, perhaps we can learn to love God amid peals of laughter.

On the one hand, we rightly think of the spiritual journey as serious business. The language of the journey is often fervent, deadly earnest. Images persist of hair shirts; long days of fasting; on your knees crawling miles to the altar, in the snow, uphill, both ways. We can remember the excesses of the ancient "pillar saints" (though I'd guess that, both now and then, awe may not be the only response of pilgrims seeing Simon Stylites sitting on a column, covered with vermin).

For many people even "joy" is serious business, a placid serenity undisturbed by grins, giggles, or guffaws. We've been helped by some writers. Richard Foster speaks of the "celebration" of discipline; Doris Donnelly writes about laughing as a "spiritual exercise." Yet instruction about spirituality generally neglects humor entirely.

One friend of mine grew up in a congregation that fiercely guarded the sacred rule, "Never laugh in church." So they didn't. Not even during the painfully long morning when a Christian drama troupe, whose main repertoire was humorous sketches, led worship. Happily, my friend was delivered from such grimness and has become the queen of post-it notes, sending messages such as "what if the hokey-pokey is really what it's all about."

On the other hand, we have humor. We think of laughter as fun, frivolous, usually entertaining. We enjoy it as a way of breaking out that you don't have to put salve on. However, we often see humor as merely frivolous. We've learned well that when you're doing something important you simply don't play around: no jokes, no wisecracks, no teasing. Surely this is one reason why children laugh twenty times more often than most adults. Life is serious, after all, and you'd better keep a straight face when you're talking about ultimate things.

The truth is that humor is fun, but it's not merely fun. It's a powerful form of communication and insight, not merely entertainment. Now I'm not turning killjoy here: "Settle down and wipe that smile off your face! Let's get serious about humor!" We can enjoy thinking about this. But we know, for example, that advertisers, full of good will as they may be, don't spend millions just to amuse us. And we've all endured personal attacks disguised as humor, followed by the stinger, "What's the matter, can't you take a joke?!" or, "Just kidding."

In a nutshell, I've become convinced that the exaggerated contrast between spirituality as somber and humor as frivolous shortchanges us. In fact, there is a wonderful interplay between humor and our spiritual journey. How we use and respond to humor tells us a lot about who we are and how we see the world. (A vital faith also shapes how we see the world and may improve our humor.) Humor even helps us see what's important and to discover fresh directions for living. It touches our relationships and shapes our personal growth. For example, humor can help us discover whether we are complete idiots or really kings and queens disguised as klutzes. It can help us sort out whether other folks are really out to get us or just bumbling, under-socialized aliens. When today's adversity crashes in on us, it can help us discern whether this is the end of the world or merely a preview of coming attractions. If the sky really is falling, humor may even serve as a hard hat to help us through.

Even if we wanted to be part of the Society of Dour Saints and use persimmon juice for communion, we still couldn't escape thinking about humor. In this media-rich culture we are bombarded by it, probably more so than at any other time in history. We've always told funny stories and joked with our friends and families, in town and tribes. Professional clowns and "fools" have prospered (or not, as the case may be) for centuries, not to mention the innocently gifted bozos we've known. But today there are also comic strips and cartoons, humorous writers, situation comedies, stand-up comics, a constant stream of funny movies and plays, and an internet flooded with jokes and parody of all sorts. Advertisers try to get us to laugh at billboards, newspaper and TV ads, and a variety of gimmicks. We are assaulted by an endless barrage of funny sayings on bumper stickers, hats, and T-shirts, not to mention clothes without words that bumble their fashion statements.

But we create this flood of humor not just for its own sake – it also serves many useful purposes. We use it to warm up social situations, to cover our uneasiness, even sometimes to make others uneasy. We joke to tell the truth and to lie, to distract each other or to get one another's attention. We use it to play, to persuade, even to persecute. We use humor in so many ways, for good and for ill, that we'll be smart to pay attention. How we respond to and use humor surely does shape our lives.

I'm assuming that you have a sense of humor, however rich, limited, or weird. Actually, it's difficult to find anyone who admits to having absolutely no sense of humor. You can probably think of a few grim folk who have tried to convince you by their actions that they have no humor, but I suspect they wouldn't confess it's extinct. Due to underuse it may have become dormant or even vestigial, but it's probably not gone. God has given us all a capacity for humor.

At the same time, a lot of people – a majority by some reports – underrate their sense of humor. They're sure they can't tell a joke or a funny story. They certainly aren't going to perform at the local comedy club and they're not the funny people whose antics and stories are the life of the party. That's fine, because having a sense of humor is much more about "being in fun" than being funny. As a matter of fact, you probably know people who are "funny" but who aren't in fun, who don't really have a sustaining sense of humor. A sense of humor is about perspective, attitude, and an undercurrent of joy and playfulness. It has much more to do with having creative tools to view and respond to our experience than with telling jokes.

Some people develop a sense of humor more naturally than others. Our personalities and experiences in our families, for example, may either foster or stifle it. Growing up in a family that rarely laughs or uses only damaging humor such as sarcasm makes it harder to be in fun. Growing up in a family filled with warm, friendly humor (as I did) makes it much easier. Predispositions, however, are not the whole story. All of us can learn and grow in the skills and perspectives of humor.

I suppose it nearly spoils the fun to say that humor is good for you – like eating your vegetables or having a regular colonoscopy. But growing a healthy sense of humor really is good for us. Since so many terrific books and articles have been written about this, I'll touch only lightly on those benefits here.

One big benefit is that humor can relieve stress. Sadly, stress so dominates modern life that most people think it's normal. A greeting card I keep handy shows a frazzled figure jumping up and down, jubilantly shouting, "I won the stress test!!" It's probably someone you know; maybe it's you. In any event, this is not a win you want. Though there is "good stress" which helps us function effectively, the prolonged, high-pitched stress that most of us face damages us physically, emotionally, and spiritually. We just can't live at "fight or flight" levels all the time.

Humor helps reduce such stress. It enables us to be flexible and to respond creatively when we're tempted to feel trapped. It gives us practical tools for perspective-taking so we can tell a bad morning from the end of the world. Hearty laughter can help restore physical and emotional balance.

Humor can also help heal us. Ever since Norman Cousins successfully used humorous videos, books, and tapes to help treat his "incurable" disease, researchers have been exploring how laughter brings healing. Cousins' classic work *Anatomy of an Illness* has spawned hundreds of scientific articles that confirm his hunches. Just as we can literally "worry ourselves sick," so also laughter can be "the best medicine." In her fun and wise book *Compassionate Laughter,* nurse Patty Wooten blends detailed explanations and medical humor to explain why. She even gives an informative and entertaining introduction to "psychoneuroimmunology" and how humor helps. I'll only give you the HMO time-limited version here. (How soon do you suppose one-day "out-patient" procedures will be offered only at drive-through stands?)

One reason humor heals is that it sets our happy hormones to bubbling, especially endorphins (the body's homemade cousin of morphine!). You probably know that endorphins are the feel-good chemicals in "runner's high." You may not know that you can get the same satisfying effect from eating half a cup of hot chili peppers. In fact, one hot pepper sauce ablaze with health warnings is called "Endorphin Rush." Happily, without sacrificing legs or gut, you can get the same benefit from some good belly laughs. And it's an experience you can easily share with your friends. You can laugh nearly anytime or any place, in any weather, and without jalapenos, special shoes, or spiffy shorts.

Studies show that laughter also lowers our blood pressure and heart rate and helps strengthen our immune systems to ward off all sorts of disease. And laughter makes you better looking. A couple of centuries ago people thought that laughter made you ugly, and even now some folks are afraid to smile, but I assure you that it will make you radiate with charm and beauty.

Why We Laugh

On our good days we think before we speak, but often we laugh before we think. Whatever happens in the brain before we laugh doesn't notify the consciousness department until it's too late.

It's only when we hear our own laughter that the screams of our better self begin to echo in our skulls: "Hey, that's not funny! What do you have for brains – oatmeal?!"

Just because we laugh before we think, however, doesn't mean we can't think after we laugh. We can scarcely snatch back our blushing, but knowing that laughter is often involuntary may help us overcome our embarrassment. Sometimes a joke will catch us off-guard, using devices like surprise or exaggeration. Sometimes it may tap into our hearts in ways we hardly expect. Nonetheless, thinking about the theories and devices of humor may help us understand.

Even though the contending theories of humor can't fully explain why we laugh, they can teach us a lot. Let's look at several of them.

One of the most popular is the relief theory. According to this view, humor is a way of throwing off the bonds of repression, of breaking free from rules and social constraints. So jokes about sex, rude behavior, and nonconformity all cry out, "Free at last! Free at last!" At least that's what Freud thought. As illustrations of this liberating stream you could also include borderline, boundary-breaking, and "naughty" humor.

An even older idea is the superiority theory, which basically insists that in order to get a laugh somebody has to get hurt. Humor needs a target, a victim. It needs to say, "I'm better than you." Clearly all kinds of in-group/out-group humor belong here, such as jokes about race, ethnicity, gender, occupation, hair color, intelligence, disabilities, and so on.

The relief and superiority theories certainly can explain a lot of the humor we encounter. Clearly, however, there is plenty to laugh about that does not grow from such negative roots, that does not require breaking boundaries or attacking someone. As we will explore in the pages that follow, God gives us the capacity for positive, healthy humor and for playful, loving laughter.

One source of this God-given humor may simply be an undercurrent of joy and playfulness. Max Eastman refers to this as simply "being in fun" and notes how innocently and easily children laugh at the puzzling and surprising things they encounter.[1] Tom Mullen recounts, for example, how his four-year-old son cracked up at the rear view of a cow walking.[2] Cows sauntering and swaying are funny for people of all ages who walk playfully through the world. Children laugh, too, as they create games and stories. But being in fun isn't just for kids. We can find joy in encountering beauty and oddity and in creating new things at any age.

Another source of humor surprised me at first, but it explains rich human experience. Dr. Christian Haggeseth suggests that our first experience of laughter comes from love, from those early moments when parent and infant look each other in the eye, smiling and laughing. And it's not just for babies. Haggeseth writes:

> When conscious eye contact is made and the setting is appropriate, the smiling human face elicits our most primitive and yet elegant humor experience.
>
> … Humor's first function in life is to convey love and security. Humor isn't just so much fluff; it is absolutely essential to human survival. It is one of the principal ways that love is expressed.[3]

What experiences of laughter do you remember growing out of love conveyed with a look and a smile? Perhaps it is a childhood experience. Perhaps it's a moment of romance when eyes and smiles met and you laughed or giggled or were nearly giddy, maybe not knowing quite why. Perhaps it's a memory of friends or even strangers. The look of love may indeed be in our eyes, and the wonder, dismay, and reassurance of it all makes us laugh. How much better the laughter of love than that of anger and hostility!

When we turn from theories of humor to the structures or devices of humor we find wide agreement. Though humorists

---

[1] Max Eastman, *Enjoyment of Laughter* (New York: Simon & Schuster, 1936), 3.
[2] Tom Mullen, *Laughing Out Loud and Other Religious Experiences* (Waco: Word Books, 1983), 23.
[3] Christian Haggeseth, *A Laughing Place* (n.p.: Berwick, 1988), 39.

describe these in great detail, I'll risk oversimplifying in a single sentence: when things don't fit, when they look funny together, we laugh – except when we're trying on bathing suits.

The funny-fit principle often takes three forms. The first is surprise. The standard joke formula uses at least two steps of misdirection to get the listener to anticipate one outcome, then the punch line suddenly shifts direction. If it's clever, we laugh. Surprises come in other forms, too – the game of peek-a-boo with youngsters, an unexpected word or idea, a pratfall, word-play, wearing a red rubber nose.

A second form of funny-fit is exaggeration. You simply can't overstate the importance of exaggeration. From ancient cave cartoons to modern stand-up comedy, exaggeration has been the first and best tool of every comic. Without blowing things way out of proportion, even to the breaking point, we'd never laugh. It's simple. When you see something that's odd or funny, make it odder still. We see it in cartoon caricatures, in the out-sized gestures and emotions of comedy, in the exaggerations we use to amuse each other when we tell stories, and in a zillion other situations.

The third form is often called incongruity, or humorous juxta-position, or absurdity. I like to call it oddmix. It's simply noticing and calling attention to things that seem odd together. It's tall and short, lean and fat, smart and dumb. It's the success of the unlikely hero, like the kid who beats the giant. It's what one of my friends calls "contradictions," which he gladly gathers. Sometimes the distance between what is and what should be is so preposterous that, even if it's tragic, we may laugh.

Understanding and using these common devices can deepen our enjoyment of humor and can help sustain, as John McKiernon puts it, "a friendly atmosphere ... creating a space where the child in us can be at home.... The humorous attitude also creates an atmosphere within which transactions of the most serious nature can take place."[4]

---

[4] John McKiernon, *Advances in Humor and Psychotherapy* (ed. William F. Fry, Jr. and Waleem J. Salameh; Sarasota, FL: Professional Resource Exchange, 1993), 190.

In the following chapters we'll look at humor in seriousness and great fun. First we'll explore how much humor intersects with our basic understandings of ourselves as humans. Then we'll consider the practical ways humor weaves itself into our daily lives of relationships, home, work, and play. We'll look at humor in the Bible and at how understanding it can heighten our enjoyment and insight, sustaining us on our journey. Finally, together we'll seek a path of holiness and hilarity, learning on the way to "enjoy God" and to serve God "with mirth."

2

The Power to Laugh

The world as we know it began, suggests Robert Farrar Capon, at a playful after-dinner bash with God the Father, Son, and Holy Spirit whopping up a huge batch of being, something the Father is just wild about. They laughed and told old jokes and threw olives and flung into existence a dazzling array of new forms of being – crocodiles and crab apples, eagles and earwigs, porcupines and platypi, and nebulae, black holes, and galaxies galore. And they kept laughing, clapping each other on the back, and shouting "Tov!" (assuming God spoke Hebrew), which in this moment meant "Wonderful!" As they began to wind down and had chuckled through the assorted humans they thought of, they shouted even louder "Tov meod!" – "Fantastic!!" While polishing off the popcorn and pistachios, they mingled "So-be-its" with "What-a-blasts!" and frequent "Amens" and it was evening and morning. What a day![1]

Capon promptly acknowledges that this is a crass analogy, noting also that crass analogies are best because no one is tempted to take them too literally. But if this scene goes over-board with its exaggeration and playfulness, it also still barely begins to portray the burst of joy and energy, love and life that set our world into being.

Dallas Willard captures a glimpse of this when he describes one of his own stunning experiences of the earth's power and beauty. "It is perhaps strange to say," he writes, "but suddenly I

---

[1] Robert Farrar Capon, *The Third Peacock* (Garden City: Doubleday, 1971), 11–12.

was extremely happy for God and thought I had some sense of what an infinitely joyous consciousness he is and of what it might have meant for him to look at his creation and find it 'very good.' "[2] He goes further: "Undoubtedly [God] is the most joyous being in the universe.... . All of the good and beautiful things from which we occasionally drink tiny droplets of soul-exhilarating joy, God continuously experiences in all their breadth and depth and richness.... . Great tidal waves of joy must constantly wash through his being."[3]

The "whirlwind speeches" of Job also give us a glimpse of God's great delight in creation and, perhaps, of the creation party itself. Even while God was laying the world's foundations and cornerstone, we are told, "the morning stars sang together and all the angels shouted for joy" (Job 38:6-7).

It makes me grin, glad but dumbfounded, to think we humans are part of the reason for all the singing and shouting. It is over us God exclaims "Tov! Tov! Tov!" as he beams over each new creature with indescribable love and joy. The world, Capon writes, "is a whole barrelful of the apples of [God's] eye, constantly juggled, relished, and exchanged by the persons of the Trinity. No wonder we love circuses, games and magic; they prove we are in the image of God."[4]

It amazes me to think that God chose to make humans in the divine image. The psalmist's words, "who are we humans that you even spare us a thought?!" speak our minds, too (compare Psalm 8:4). What surprise! What incongruity! What laughter! Too-good-to-be-true laughter, to be sure – but, preposterous as it may seem, humans bear God's likeness. Whatever else that image-bearing means, surely it means that we can love and choose, that we can collaborate with God in governing the world with tender care and delight, and that we can create endlessly.

Our powers to create scarcely match God's, but we haven't even begun to exhaust them. We build tall-mast schooners and

---

[2] Dallas Willard, *The Divine Conspiracy* (New York: HarperSan-Francisco, 1998), 63.

[3] Willard, *Divine Conspiracy*, 62–63.

[4] Capon, *Third Peacock*, 14.

space shuttles; we write poems and business plans, software and symphonies; we paint watercolors and improvise twelve-bar blues. And we play with words, tell jokes, draw cartoons, invent games, banter and play in all sorts of ways to express and enjoy the wonder of our great creative gift.

Creating and enjoying humor help us live gladly as people made in God's image. Humor displays and delights in our basic nature and powers and shares God's own joyous being. Rather than looking on soberly and disapprovingly, I'd venture that God laughs, too, at our clever stories and bad puns, even enjoying (or especially enjoying) our bumbling attempts – much as we enjoy young children learning to tell jokes and riddles. Our joy and laughter simply emulate God's delight in the world. We're made for humor – and God likes it.

Being in fun

Though we'll talk about creating humor, it's even more important to emphasize that we really don't have to work hard to enjoy humor. For most of us it has more to do with relaxing a bit rather than working at it. Trying harder will probably just make us like the folks who get uptight about the things they do to relax – golf, tennis, synchronized surgery, whatever. If we loosen our grip and let our natural playfulness bubble to the surface, we can learn to enjoy again the habit of "being in fun."

"Being in fun" comes naturally to children, who have not yet hidden or twisted this gift from God. Researchers have discovered that babies and young children laugh often but that, as we grow older, we laugh less and less. Apparently the burdens of sophistication, of self-importance, of the pace of life rob us of laughter until, collectively, we're about as funny as cold oatmeal.

In his entertaining book *Laughing Out Loud and Other Religious Experiences*, Tom Mullen enjoys recounting how children remind us of the gift of being in fun – laughing easily at things slightly askew, at random mishaps (if they don't hurt), at grown-ups flashing funny faces in games of peekaboo, at a world full of oddity and fun.[5] When we live in a spirit of playfulness, we will see a torrent of funny stuff right under our noses. We might even begin with our noses.

Of course, we know you can get old without growing up, but can't we also grow up without getting grim? It is not better to curse a candle than to light the darkness. It is not okay to be cantankerous and dour. We don't have to analyze everything. We don't have to attribute Deep Meaning to all the details of life. And certainly we don't have to live continually in crisis, addicted to adrenaline, the hysterical hormone. Besides, it's not good for you. I think I read somewhere (you expect a footnote on this?) that if you overdose on adrenaline in your twenties and thirties, when you're fifty your adrenal cortex crumbles and falls out of your skull, leaving you three short steps from brain-dead. Obviously this is a lay paraphrase of serious science, but trust me on this. Cruising through life in crisis is not good for you. It's better to pump endorphins than adrenaline. Having a laugh beats having a coronary. Hoot when you can; there's plenty of crisis to go around. Don't court trouble; let lying dogs sleep.

Consider instead the habit of "being in fun." It's simply being ready to enjoy life's incongruities. It's being predisposed to be amused (sometimes amazed) rather than annoyed. If we can sustain playfulness and innocence, watching cows walking is only the beginning of entertainment. (Fans of Gary Larson's *The Far Side* may chuckle again now at his images of cows standing around, smoking cigarettes and talking, ready to warn one another when humans approach to put out their smokes and resume standing on all fours.) Simple things, like what people wear, often make me laugh – though rarely out loud. Kindness counts, too. It amuses (and amazes) me to think that most people you see actually choose to dress the way they do! (There are exceptions, of course. I am told that many women, rightly or wrongly, are convinced that the men in their lives can't possibly

---

[5] Tom Mullen, *Laughing Out Loud*, 24.

choose the right shirt or find matched socks, so they always tell them what to wear. Sometimes, I'd guess, they dress them badly just for laughs, or spite. I, a semi-capable man, dress myself – though I sometimes suspect this makes it easier for others to be in fun.)

Making Humor

Being in fun helps us to enjoy the funny things that unfold right in front of us, but we can do more. Sometimes we need to try to have fun. The possibilities are endless.

One way to have fun is simply to play. Play games of all sorts, juggle, kick a hacky sack. Even sports can be fun rather than ego-wars. Take, for instance, my love of basketball. I laugh a lot and my teammates often find my skills amusing. In one of Bill Cosby's early monologues he describes trying to run a figure-eight play in basketball only to complete a figure-three. I know that play. In my case, I can't remember the second part of two-part plays: give and go, pick and roll, though not run and gun. I give and watch, pick and stand (and grin). It's the complexity, I guess. I can't even get bulimia right. It's just binge, binge, binge.

We can sing silly songs, including those great camp songs where you get to improvise verses. We can read funny stories aloud together. Even before we had kids, my wife Margi and I used to read Winnie the Pooh together until we cried laughing. For us it's the same with Patrick McManus' *The Good Samaritan Strikes Again* (and many others) or John McPherson's *Close to Home* cartoons.

Maybe even better are serial stories in which one person starts making up a story, the next person continues it, and so on. A friend tells me his children love this story game, but it's not just for kids. Adults who spin serial stories or act through the surprises of improv have just as much fun.

Let me suggest, too, that you collect humor. If you see or think of something that really makes you laugh, write it down, clip it, throw it in a folder, tape it in a scrapbook or journal, frame it. In some way save it to enjoy again, to share with friends, or to pull out on a not-so-funny day.

Play sometimes involves making humor. For example, when we get into imaginative games of "what if ..." and keep adding comic twists and layers to a funny premise, we're creating humor. We can do the same in playful banter as we ping-pong ideas, puns and non sequiturs back and forth to each other. It's great fun, for example, when my colleague Paul and I spontaneously fall into an idea romp, careening playfully through topics biblical, theological, nonsensical, and beyond. After a few minutes we declare again our alter egos "Jot and Tittle, the Bible Answer Persons," and slip back into our offices and, of course, deep thought.

Humor also comes from putting things together in new and surprising ways. Sometimes you discover unexpected mixes simply by staying tuned to the funny stuff that happens in your head while you're doing something else. My own cerebral compost heap, for example, sprouted a new idea while our church choir was rehearsing a fine anthem by Ken Bible. I had a vision of matching that fine name with the Ain't-It-Precious Wide-eyed Bible for kids – and producing the new Ken and Barbie Study Bible. I hope you don't mind if it still amuses me. (Note to Mattel and Zondervan or whomever: this idea is protected by copyright and I'll be happy to negotiate royalties with you if you'll protect my reputation from further damage.)

Sometimes we consciously work at funny new word combinations – like when we create puns or "Tom Swifties" or other wordplay. ("I hope I can still play the guitar," Tom fretted. "I feel like a big black bird," Tom crowed.) I enjoy using familiar formulae from our culture and finishing them in new ways. For instance, I'm thinking of sending a copy of *Soteriology for Dummies*, a much-needed book, to the library of the Home for Hoary Heretics. (Even you can do better than that.)

We can physically make funny things with pictures, paint, clay, or potatoes. I loved the Potato Head family as a kid, and was constantly trying out new arrangements of eyes, ears, and lips. Now, in addition to potatoes and clay, you can also create with computers. Graphics programs and games offer myriad possibilities for doctoring photos and creating entirely new and amusing critters of our own. Of course, we're bordering here also on the not-so-playful, but sometimes funny, possibilities of genetic manipulation. I suppose it is already possible, for example, to add genetic material from fireflies to human DNA, thus creating families whose buttocks glow in the dark. (My friend Shannon suggests that they be invited to evening barbecues, I suppose for light entertainment.)

We can create humor by just making things up. Write jokes, funny essays or stories, comedy sketches, stand-up routines, tall tales. Or plan and pull off playful (but harmless, please) pranks. I won't detail examples here except to say to Jaylene, wherever you are: turning the great clock tower on Davis Hall into a Mickey Mouse watch the night before university board meetings is still one of the best.

Creative play – in the form of games or pranks, banter, jokes or stories – lets our God-likeness shine through. It brightens our lives but also witnesses to the love and joyousness of our Creator. To fail to enjoy it would be to belittle the truth about our gifts and powers.

Humor and Creativity

This gift of creating humor has a further dimension, for humor itself can also stimulate our creativity. Laughter and play jump-start our creative powers. That's why a lot of creativity consultants in the business world, for example, include games and humor in their secret arsenal. But the secret is out.

The technical explanation runs like this. When laughter strikes, it frees little creative messengers in the brain who have been marching lockstep, sober-faced, trying to squeeze out a good idea. Now all of a sudden they're like kids at recess. They run around every which way, chasing each other, playing tag, concocting surprises, laughing, spraying "what if" chemicals on unsuspecting parts of the cerebral cortex, and generally creating an atmosphere of controlled chaos where really interesting things can happen.

Doug Hall, who modestly identifies himself as "Retired Master Marketing Inventor" and "creator of the Eureka!® Stimulus Response Method™" insists that "fun is fundamental" to creativity. He insists: "You might as well try surviving for a week without oxygen as create without fun."[6] In the same vein, creativity whiz Roger Von Oech explains, "I'll bet that you generate most of your new ideas when you are playing in your mental playground. That's because your defenses are down, your mental locks are loosened, and there is little concern with the rules, practicality, or being wrong."[7] Humor and fun supercharge creativity.

Doug Hall works with top marketing and research executives, often from big-name companies, to help them maximize their "productive creativity." Whether at his Eureka!® Mansion or on the road, he uses an array of unconventional tools to create an environment of fun, to recapture childlike innocence and wonder, and to rekindle imaginative thinking. His tool kit includes toys and games of all sorts, bubbles and kazoos, Nerf weapons and squirt guns, Play-Doh and crayons, and, neither last nor least, whoopee cushions. He seems especially buoyant in remembering the occasion of his first "gang whoopee" in which 132 top executives sat in unison to create a "mighty buh-rrrrraaappppp!"[8] The out-of-the-box stunt helped to release great energy and creativity in that group for the rest of the week.

At one level play and laughter need to be pointless, but at another level the point is that they reflect who we are, and they get results. Studies conducted by Dr. Arthur Van Gundy at the University of Oklahoma showed that Hall's approach, compared to traditional approaches, generated dramatically more

---

[6] Doug Hall and David Wecker, *Jump Start Your Brain* (New York: Warner Books, 1995), 9.

[7] Roger von Oech, *A Whack on the Side of the Head* (New York: Warner, 1983), 97.

[8] Hall and Wecker, *Jump Start*, 33.

ideas in a session, and a much higher percentage of useable ideas. In addition, participants were much more satisfied with the experience.[9] Clearly humor stimulates creativity. Again, in Hall's words, "There's no category or creative challenge that can't be improved by making it more fun."[10]

We can experiment with applying this insight ourselves and in groups we're part of, whether committees or working units. I've seen the benefits of humor in my academic department (motto: "Pray and Play") even though we've been less intentional than Hall. I've also giggled a bit about the prospect of applying these principles full-scale to the meetings of a church's board of elders. To be fair, not all such groups are humor-impaired, but you might have fun imagining Hall working with one of the no-nonsense, never-crack-a-smile groups you know. Even now I'm relishing the idea of turning him loose on the United States Senate.

My own experience as a student and a teacher confirms that humor also enhances creativity and learning in the classroom. Educators Diane Loomans and Karen Kolberg remind us that in "a laughing classroom ... the walls expand, the ceiling lifts, differences begin to dissolve, and a tremendous sense of 'mental mobility' abounds... . Outrageous streaks of genius emerge without self-consciousness, and both the teacher and the learner become receptive to exploring new possibilities."[11]

Not only in business and education, but also in science, technology, medicine, the arts, personal problem-solving, and much more, the point is clear. Laughter and play liberate our God-given creative powers.

The themes we've explored here are great news – especially for those who have been deceived into thinking that the spiritual journey must be grim duty, dull and lifeless. God has shared great joy and creative powers with us and God wants us,

---

[9] Hall and Wecker, *Jump Start*, 90–94.
[10] Hall and Wecker, *Jump Start*, 329.
[11] Diane Loomans and Karen Kolberg, *The Laughing Classroom* (Tiburon: H.J. Kramer, 1993), 32.

in turn, to share them with one another. In our creativity we delight to make each other laugh and boost our powers to create all the more. Glad laughter is a great way to thank God.

3

The Klutz Factor

My barber fancies himself a specialist in contradictions. He catches the government making laws that bounce back on themselves. He remembers when they raised taxes to repair a local school and used the money to tear it down. And he can spot hypocrites at one hundred paces – people who sometimes fail to live up to their values or who make promises they don't intend to keep. Each time I visit he has new contradictions to joke about. I laugh; he's caught them again. But so far I haven't had the heart to tell him that, though he's good at it, it's not that hard.

The truth is, we're full of contradictions. Really smart people, like you and me, do really stupid things. Again and again. And again. We walk proud and erect only to fall down the stairs. For health's sake we eat sensibly all day only to do unspeakable things late at night with peanut butter. (Or chocolate chip cookie dough. Or a tub of ice cream. You can work it out from here, but quit drooling.) We take a grand bow only to discover we're unzipped. Our whispered wisecracks nearly thunder in a room fallen suddenly silent. We know that Murphy's Law, "anything that can go wrong will go wrong," is true along with its corollary, "Murphy was an optimist."

Contradictions are everywhere, and they provide an endless supply of humor. When asked whether some seasons are more fun for humor writers, Scott Dikkers, the editor of the newspaper parody magazine *The Onion* observed: "The truth is, every season is pretty fun for us. If humans stop doing stupid things, we'll have a tougher time finding things to write about. But what are the chances of that happening? I think our jobs are pretty safe for now."[1]

I call all of this the Klutz Factor. Embedded in the magnificent powers and possibilities that women and men have is a tendency for klutziness. We don't invite it, but it shows up anyway. We hate it, but we also celebrate it.

We laugh gladly at the follies of others, and sometimes even at our own. We relish stories of stupid crooks, for example, who shove bank tellers a note, "Give me all your money," scribbled on the back of their own deposit slips. We also love stories of incompetent cheaters like the student who, in copying his neighbor's exam response, "I can't answer that," wrote, "I can't answer that either."

We are astonished and amused at stories gathered for the Darwin Awards, which celebrate, posthumously, people whose stupidly self-destructive behavior has done the most to eliminate undesirable elements from the human gene pool. The stories are numerous, many now classic. For example, there's the fellow who strapped a jet engine to his car without thinking about how to slow down or shut it off until he was airborne and approaching a cliff at a gazillion miles per hour. Or the guy who was trying to catch fish by stunning them with M-250 firecrackers (illegal in his native Illinois, of course) and blew a hole in the bottom of his aluminum rowboat – and couldn't swim. And there's the zookeeper who didn't live through his solo attempt to relieve one of his elephants of life-threatening constipation. (I can't give details here in this more-or-less polite book, but you can easily find these stories and others on the internet.)

I'm all of a sudden a bit uncomfortable to see that I've only told stories about stupid men. Evenhandedness requires that we at least admit the possibility that both women and men may have outbreaks of klutziness, both small and great. We can all lock the keys in the car, forget appointments, or, when introducing a dear friend, forget her name. To give full credit, women can

---

[1] *Yahoo* (16 May 2000), 145.

commit big gaffes, too. For example, how about the woman who won a million dollars in the lottery with a ticket she had bought with a stolen credit card? (It belonged to her deceased mother-in-law!) Last I knew, she was in jail and the police were trying to find where she'd stashed the first $30,000 winner's payout.

The Klutz Factor may actually be built into human life. On the one hand, we have great powers; on the other, we are limited by design. Though we can create, we are still creatures. Though we are made in the image of God, we are not God. (Sorry.) Still we stretch to grasp things beyond our reach and, tiptoe on the top rung, we often fall off the ladder. The serpent in the Garden of Eden tempted humans with the promise, "Eat from the forbidden tree and you will be like God." We still fall for that promise, heady with our powers and chafing under our limits.

Here humor really helps. Laughing at our own klutziness makes a lot of sense, even beyond beating other folks to the first laugh. For one thing it helps us keep perspective, especially when we're tempted to get uppity. It reminds us of our true humanity, wonder and warts included. Probably you've noticed that arrogance stifles humor. It's hard to laugh when you're ten feet above contradiction. After all, being important is not a laughing matter! Which, of course, makes it all the more fun for humble folks like us to lance pomposity and bombast with humor.

Laughing can also remind us that we don't have to be perfekt. Now if you really were perfect, the rest of us would have to hate you; if you pretended to be perfect, we'd all just laugh at you. But the good new is that you can't be, ever. We can be perfectly wonderful or perfectly awful. We can be terrific, really good, even good enough, but not perfect.

Accepting that we have a klutz chromosome frees us up. For one thing, we can be gentler with ourselves (and with others), tempering our failures and disappointments with humor rather than with anger and self-condemnation. We'll say more about timeliness later, but certainly there are times when laughter cannot and should not come easily or quickly. Still we're often better off to laugh in our embarrassment, to use humor to frame our disappointments. It's a way of picking ourselves up when we fall, dusting ourselves off, and continuing the journey.

Accepting the fact of limitation also frees us to be playful, to enjoy the world more fully. We can try new things, for example, without having to be good at them. As G.K. Chesterton once said, "Anything worth doing is worth doing badly."

For example, early on, when learning to play the guitar, sore fingers and forgotten chords can be more amusing than annoying – though that may pass. Or consider genuinely righteous folk who never learned to dance. Should they turn to such wickedness, they might better laugh than blush. Occasionally I have attempted moves remotely like dance, but, given my size and agility, observers have viewed this as antisocial dancing and laughed. So have I.

Enjoy the mistakes, the contradictions, and the funny mix of things right around you. They're so common that it almost forces us to show more compassion toward ourselves and others. We're always bumping into human limits and incongruity. Walking through my neighborhood, for example, I always chuckle at the house with big "welcome" and smiley-face signs right next to a large black-and-orange notice, "Beware of dog!" The bumper stickers on a beater truck down the street also amuse me. One urges Bible reading, another greater patriotism, a third brags on being Scottish, and a fourth reads, "Blow it out your bagpipes!" I also enjoy misspellings on panel vans, in newspapers, and sometimes in student papers. (I can't tell you how often students have written about women "baring children" or the Israelites "wondering" in the wilderness.)

I'm always on the lookout for new church "bulletin bloopers" (like, for example, the one announcing meetings to be held in the "perish hall") and "news of the weird." Of course, sometimes bloopers happen right under your nose. I wish I had been present at my church, for example, when a former pastor, hoping to impress his visiting family with the congregation's singing, urged, "Let's all stand and sing lustfully!" Reliable witnesses tell me that, after a stunned silence, laughter rolled in waves from the choir over the whole congregation. I did witness, however, the gaffe of a friend proudly presiding at his daughter's wedding. He enthusiastically invited us to sing, "All hail the power of Jesus' name, let angels prostate fall." To his chagrin, the videotape trumped his post-ceremony denials. Occasionally I'll clip an article or record one of these in a notebook. It's fun to see them again and to share them with friends. But, frankly, such examples are so common that there's always a fresh supply.

I also invite you to notice and laugh when you bump against your own limitations. It's a simple way to know and accept ourselves more fully. It also gets us closer to reality, which is a lot like being closer to humility. As Thomas Merton wrote, "humility consists in being precisely the person you actually are before God."[2] The word "humble" actually grows out of the word *"humus,"* which refers to earth or the ground. Based on this root word, then, to humble oneself (or to be humiliated, another path to humility) is to get low or close to the ground. Yet this also suggests the kind of authenticity Merton advocates. It's to be down to earth, to recognize that we are creatures, God-molded dust into whom God has gladly breathed life. If I could rewrite the history of English, I'd get humor, humble, humus, humming, and humbug all from the same fictional Indo-European root *hum-.* But, sadly, I have to admit that "humor" comes from a different root that has to do with liquids and temperament. Etymology aside, however, humor is a wonderful way to get down to earth. It can gently, even playfully, challenge the pretense that distorts our lives.

Laughing at ourselves need not be harsh or embarrassing. My brother Mauri (deservedly my favorite musician) learned this from an older man playing the violin as dinner music at a banquet. While playing enthusiastically and joyfully, he occasionally made a mistake, a chill-your-spine squawk. Yet, instead of showing a flash of anger or crippling embarrassment, the

---

[2] Thomas Merton, *New Seeds of Contemplation* (New York: New Directions, 1961), 99.

violinist gently laughed out loud and continued playing with the same joyous enthusiasm. Mauri tells me that gentle laugh shed new light on the burden of musical perfection, opening ways to create with joy but without fear.

Growing to understand and accept ourselves, to know we are accepted, klutzy and limited as we are, is vital to the spiritual journey. Chuckles, giggles, and guffaws can help us on the way.

An Imperfect Measure

Having limits is not in itself a moral flaw. At the same time, listening to how we use humor in responding to limits may well give us clues about our progress in the spiritual journey. Since humor is complex, I can only guarantee the listening tool I suggest below to about 99% accuracy. After all, what we laugh at and what humor we create may be influenced by social settings and old habits. Still, how we use humor often reveals habits of the heart. Let me suggest, then, a simple but imperfect measure, a listening tool, based on a continuum with anger and hostility at one end and acceptance and embrace at the other. Please understand that this tool is still in its pre-scientific stages; it doesn't use decimal points (though, apart from money, I think numbers with decimal points are over-rated). However, the method is clear: simply pay attention to the humor you use and enjoy, then decide where it belongs on this scale.

At one end of the continuum, we can respond to human limitation with anger. We really do want "life without limits," as teaser titles suggest. This is literally true. The chilling reality is that there are people today who pay big bucks to be frozen for a century or so, or for however long it takes to cure human mortality. If there are no major power outages or natural disasters, they may eventually be thawed ("under new management") once scientists have perfected the treatment for frostbite. I bet they'll be mad (or is that "frosted"?) to discover that they didn't buy out of mortality.

None of us can overcome the klutz chromosome, but the illusion of perfection, of the possibility that we just might beat the limits, lingers. This illusion often spawns anger, hostility, and intolerance toward others who are imperfect – and even toward ourselves. Even self-deprecating humor can bear this angry tone. What we reject in others we can also reject in ourselves.

In many cases, no doubt, anger and rebellion against limits are the weeds that grow out of the deep root of fear. We're not sure, given limits, that we'll have what we need, that we can find the joy that calls to us. Or, more boldly, we're mad and scared that we won't. The temptation scene in the Garden of Eden, where the serpent successfully accuses God of not having the best interests of humans at heart, suggests how deeply this touches us. This fear, too, easily masks itself as anger and moves to hostile humor.

Whatever form it may take – insult, ridicule, or sarcasm, for example – hostile humor is sharp and potentially devastating, even though it may be really funny. Some comics (like Don Rickles, "you hockey puck!") have based their careers on barbed humor. And many forms of public comedy today rely on ridicule in some form, often framed in ways that draw us to laugh at (and indirectly own) things we'd be horrified to say ourselves. Where insecurity, fear, and anger flourish, insult jokes are an easy way to get a laugh. What does our easy laughter, though, reveal about our hearts?

On the other end of the continuum is acceptance. It embraces, even celebrates, that we are creatures. The humor of acceptance gathers us together, chuckling over the fact that we're all in the same boat, that we share limitation, and that it's okay. "Isn't it awful?! Isn't it grand?! Isn't it to laugh!?"

Some of our favorite humorists – people like Will Rogers, Bill Cosby, Erma Bombeck, and Charles Schulz – draw us in with this comedy of embrace. They share our humanity, making us laugh together at our quirks and foibles, our glory and our klutziness. They help us see that it's funny and it's okay that we all run out of gas, spill the milk, say the exact wrong thing, and have episodes of grandiosity.

Ultimately the laughter of acceptance may tell us that on the spiritual journey we have also embraced trust and grace. Once we relax into the truth that God's love for us is without catch or limit and that the God who generously provides for wildflowers and sparrows will also care for us, our laughter changes. The laughter of fear and resentment becomes the laughter of abundance and dreams come true. Klutzy as we are, we are still the apples of God's eye. Yee-haw. Tee-hee.

4

Center of the Universe

One of the drawbacks of trying to be Center of the Universe is that it's so crowded there. Lots of folks shove and tug, climb and clamor to be at the center. Each one passionately believes that he or she should be in charge, that he or she is the sun around which all else revolves. At the opening of each episode of the animated cartoon *Pinky and the Brain*, featuring two laboratory mice, Pinky asks, "What are we going to do tonight, Brain?" Brain replies impatiently, "The same thing we do every night, Pinky. We're going to take over the world!"

Being Director of the Universe, as Loretta LaRoche calls it, poses daunting challenges. But most of us, in our heart of hearts, believe we're up to it. We know that if everyone would just do things our way, evil would soon be vanquished; the cosmos itself would bask in the glow of peace; stupidity and taxes would end; and everyone would sing gladly of our benevolence and wisdom. Well, at least we would be happy.

This is how the Bible describes what has gone wrong. In the Garden of Eden the serpent closed the sale with humans when he whispered, "And you will be like God. You get to be in charge. Everything will revolve around and depend on you. You'll finally have what you deserve – power, control, adoration, and the right to sing 'I did it my way'" (Genesis 3:5). It's a sure-fire sales pitch that still tempts us all. It's also the root of sin. We noted earlier that it's not a moral flaw to be a creature, to have limits. But a moral problem results when the creature tries to usurp the place of the Creator. The job of Director of the Universe is already taken.

This is also where a lot of comedy begins. Certainly sin has tragic consequences, but it also has the structures of the comic. An exaggerated sense of one's place and powers leads inevitably to pretense and pomposity, to the ludicrous and absurd. We're sure to enjoy an unfailing stream of laughter since, in our never-ending game of King of the Hill, we love using humor to puncture others inflated self-images. After all, they're in our place.

Symptoms of Self-Centering

The word "symptoms" tells you flat out that I'm treating this like a disease. Actually, it's an epidemic – and we all know a lot of victims. It's easy to diagnose in others, though it's harder to see the symptoms in ourselves. What are some of the danger signs?

C.W. Metcalf gives what he calls the "top-three warning signs" of Center-of-the-Universe behavior. They all have to do with "fault." They are: "Number 3: *Nothing* is *ever* your *fault*... . Number 2: *Everything* is *always* your *fault*... . Number 1: Any combination of 2 and 3 above."[1] My wise wife Margi insists wryly that you've solved the problem when you can identify who's at fault. If someone else messed up (and, of course, didn't act as splendidly as we would have), then we can still hold onto the illusions of superiority and control. If, on the other hand, things happen for good or ill because of us, then we prove that we have effective power. Metcalf recalls a 1960s-style young woman, "Fly Fire," who believed her moods dictated the weather: her sadness brought rain and her gladness bright sunshine. (I suspect that a lot of farmers would be glad to make her sad.)

A separate but related symptom to "fault" is the idea of responsibility. Some folks know that it's their destiny, their

---

[1] C.W.A. Metcalf and Roma Felible, *Lighten Up: Survival Skills for People Under Pressure* (Reading: Perseus Books, 1993), 70ff.

sometimes dreadful responsibility, to make sure that the world stays on its axis, that gravity works, and that the seasons arrive on time. Some of them are really good at it. They observe and evaluate, order and organize all in their path. They have the gift of knowing how things should be and they're generous in sharing this knowledge, realizing how eager we all are for their wisdom. What they can't oversee, they can worry about. Each of them is the Director of the Universe on the prowl.

Hyper-responsibility and controlling behaviors, of course, also lead to empire-building. It doesn't take much. The guy in my college dorm who had the keys to the vending machine wanted not only courtesy but also minor acts of worship before he'd help recover lost coins. My wife worked with a veteran secretary who transformed clerical work into an autocracy by gradually installing a quirky and secret filing system. Using her secrets to blackmail her superiors eventually let her mostly eat and watch others work. (She probably wished she'd been filing that one day during the Christmas season when she ate most of the office party's sugar plums!)

Sometimes it's worse. Gossip group gurus, cult leaders, and revolutionaries large and small grow cadres of followers who are True Believers, who have the inside scoop, who know they're the best, who need to "take over the world."

People of such importance deserve respect, of course, and often demand that they get it. Perhaps they'll insist on perks and parking places or salaries and titles befitting their status. Address them properly ("That's 'Your Most Excellent Mucky-Muck,' son, but you may call me 'Sir.'"). Show a little deference. Don't contradict, giggle, or get in the way. Certainly don't "disrespect" them.

I sometimes forget. I recall with mixed chagrin and laughter a moment of high stupidity when I embarrassed the boss in public. (Should they read this, I can imagine each of several bosses thinking he's the one I'm writing about. He probably is.) Upstaging your "betters" is not a good career move. Yet, as my family well knows, being constantly right is a hard burden for me to bear.

An equal but opposite strain of Center-of-the-Universe-itis to that suffered by young "Fly Fire," who made everything happen, manifests itself when everything that happens is *about* you. You are the focus. It's personal. The baby deposits her lunch on your sweater in order to ruin your day. The rain comes to spoil your picnic. They hiked gas prices to coincide with your vacation. Or, more cheerfully, the fish are biting just to make your day.

Still another evidence of Center-of-the-Universe behavior is sheer oblivion. The oblivious act as if there is no one else in the universe. We know these people. They drive hell-bent on busy roads, act shocked when they crash into our shopping carts, knock us aside while retrieving their luggage, yell into their cell phones at the coffee shop, and embarrass the world with unrestrained public displays of affection. And they don't know anybody's there. Center of the Universe gives way to I Am the Universe.

Sometimes we even drag God in on this behavior, supposing that God's sole purpose in the universe is to make us happy and that God is busy arranging people, happenstances, and parking places for that purpose. Certainly God intends great joy for each of us and is intimately involved with our lives, but the Bible suggests that God is even more interested in having a whole cosmos full of people and critters, each glad to take its God-given place, all get along and party together in peace (see, for example, Isaiah 11:1-9; 25:6-8; 65:17-25).

Challenges of Self-Centering

As we've seen, being the Center of the Universe isn't easy. While it's easy to spot why others aren't up to the job, we can hardly spot the flaws in our own performance on the job. We can easily deceive ourselves and be deceived. The Director of the Universe can be duped. Of course to grasp at such power means that we've already bought the serpent's lie and lied to ourselves. But hangers-on may help sustain the illusion. They'll fawn and flatter and nod in agreement, maybe even buy our lunch, hoping to be seated in authority at our right hand.

Medieval courts used humor to challenge such deceptions. Kings kept court jesters, or "fools," whose job was to parody and challenge every plan. Playfulness, exaggeration, and ridicule might make stupidity show its true colors when ring-kissing courtiers would not. It was a smart institution, I think, though a risky career for performers who any night might die on stage.

Another challenge of serving as Director is that it takes enormous energy and guarantees an industrial-size supply of frustration and disappointment. No matter how hard we try, most other folks just can't get it right. So, because we are responsible, we have to work even harder and grab for even more control so we can make sure things turn out okay. It is, of course, annoying and grossly unfair that we have to do everything ourselves – but someone has to do it!

It's also a constant struggle to sustain the image of sophistication and invincibility that befits a Director. The right clothes might help, I suppose. (Do you remember "power ties?" I keep one for special occasions but suspect it's now the wrong color and size.) Probably demeanor counts more – the walk, how you carry yourself, your manner, self-confidence, nose height, coolness, and so on. Maintaining a convincing image while walking through the minefield of people ready to take potshots and usurp our position can just wear us out!

You've probably noticed another challenge that faces people who suffer from being the Center of the Universe: their humor is messed up. Sometimes they are so stressed and pompous (responsibility and image issues again) that they have no humor at all. Which is often pretty funny. Henri Bergson got it right: "the one failing that is essentially laughable is vanity."[2]

They may have humor that's more a weapon than a toy, humor without the fun. One recent study of humor in the office,

---

[2] Elton Trueblood, *The Humor of Christ* (New York: Harper & Row, 1964), 37.

for example, concluded that while women use humor to build relationships and lower stress, men use it as a tool of competition. Predictably, trading "zingers" and put-down humor to gain advantage increases stress and damages relationships. The article, as I recall, was written by a woman (women are gifted in these matters, you know), though I know of women who gladly play such "men's" games.

Stepping Away from the Center

An engaging image on postcards and T-shirts shows the Milky Way, white on a black background. An arrow points to a spot near the edge of the galaxy, with the legend "You are here." The postcard fine print goes on to explain that our sun is "only one of 200 billion stars in the Milky Way galaxy" and there are "at least 100 billion other galaxies." Oh! The few billion more than I'd counted on makes playing Director really hard.

C.W. Metcalf proposes a less cosmic but very practical device for perspective building, which I've found helpful. Take a sheet of paper and label it "The Known Universe." In the middle of the paper write "Center," and in a corner write "Me." I've tried another version to make the ludicrous obvious. How does it feel to write "Me" in the middle and "You" in a corner? I felt stupid. Such a visual sticks in the memory pretty well, but we can easily recreate it whenever we get confused on this principle. When this seems hard, it could be a sign that it's time to explore why.

Another way for us to step away from being Director is to nurture an alternate view of ourselves, a more authentic view. Of course, don't be improperly modest.

If the world's welfare does indeed rest on you, you'll just have to own up to it. Barring that, though, we can all work on realism.

The Apostle Paul urges Christians to have an accurate self-understanding, one tempered by knowing what God is doing in us (Romans 12:3-6,10). Good "spiritual friends" can help us do that. So can a vital life of prayer, which steadily reveals and refines who we really are.

Laughing at ourselves can help, too. It can prod us to see ourselves more realistically and less respectably, which is a real advantage. Learning to laugh at our own "bloopers" and embarrassing moments, for example, helps undercut delusions of grandeur. Metcalf (again) suggests slipping into a photo booth and creating silly pictures of yourself to keep in your wallet or hide in your organizer. (My family has an ample supply of such photos already.) A lot of us can just use our driver's license photos. Sneaking a peek at funny mug shots can help us get a grip when we're hyperventilating about making sure gravity works.

We can take ourselves more lightly, too, by joking (gently) about personal traits that might embarrass us – personality quirks, body size or shape, noses, hair (curly, straight, gone), varieties of derangement. Outside my favorite coffee shop I recently saw a large man on a mountain bike who was wearing a T-shirt that urged in huge letters "GET FAT." It was advertising bike tires, I learned, but I identified with his sense of humor. (I'm way ahead in my battle against anorexia.) It also reminds me of the guy with a shirt that read, "I have the body of a god. Sadly, it's Buddha." Gentle humor about ourselves can guide us toward accepting ourselves as we are, follies and foibles included, just as God does.

A couple of writers promote the value of laughing at yourself in a mirror (naked even!). This is weird, though I think it might work. (Don't send pictures.) I do know that lightening up your environment helps combat Center-of-the-Universe impulses, and it can be very simple. In my office, for example, I keep a stuffed Benedictine monk with a red nose (a fabric toy, silly), a portrait of "Tut-ankh-newman" (a Middle Kingdom Egypt treatment of *Mad* magazine's hero), a tile plaque a friend brought me from Jerusalem that reads "Dung Gate," a stash of red foam rubber noses to give away and use as needed, and other assorted images and toys that make me smile. At home, where I can be even less respectable, I enjoy a humor library chock-full of cartoons, stories, videos, music, and tapes; a mugging and winking "Mona Lisa" that makes me laugh every time; and other treasures to grin for. By the time this book is published I may even have learned how to juggle.

Now I take all this frivolity very seriously. Lightening up fights our distortions and lifts the crushing, yet enticing, burden of being the Center of the Universe.

The New Testament says a lot about this, too – in one place, for example, through the sad and comical story about Jesus' disciples quarreling over who was the greatest. They were even sneaking around (with special pleading from Mom!) trying to get Jesus to give them the advantage. Surely they blushed (do you suppose some chuckled?) when Jesus called them on it and told them that the point was not lording it over others, but serving others (Matthew 20:20-28). Here, and elsewhere, the pervasive New Testament message of mutual submission and mutual service makes a full frontal assault on clawing our way to the top. Service, rightly given, breaks pomposity's power and need not be grinding duty. No doubt we've all seen huffy, demanding "servants" – and laughed because it's so odd. Robert Holden, founder of the NHS Laughter Clinic in Birmingham, England, gets it right when he says, "Give yourself away today. Be of service to the world today.... . People who live joyfully tend to live generously. They have it worked out for themselves that giving does not diminish them: it enriches them."[3]

The reversals here and in Jesus' words seem almost comic, don't they? Give and get; die and live; to be great, serve; the first will be last and the last first. That seems to be a funny way to run a universe; if we were in charge, things wouldn't be that way. But we're not, and they are. Such foolishness, Paul insists, beats our wisdom (1 Corinthians 1:20-31). Well what do you know?!

---

[3] Robert Holden, *Laughter the Best Medicine* (London: Thorsons, 1993), 129.

Part II
Walking Cheerfully Day to Day

5

Sneaky Truth, Sneaky Lies

We have already noted that we usually laugh before we think. It's okay to laugh first; that's how humor works. Devices like surprise, exaggeration, reversals, and funny pairings, for example, often trigger our laugh sensors while sneaking around our mental fortresses. Just because we laugh before we think, however, doesn't mean we can't think after we laugh. It's too late to grab back the cackle, but it's not too late to think.

Humor, like parables, gets through to us by catching us off guard. While we're intently defending the front door, humor sneaks in the back, gets a snack out of the fridge, and makes itself at home. We might not even notice for a while that humor is hogging the couch and playing with our mind. But eventually we'll have to deal with it.

Obviously, sneaking around the first line of defense is a great strategy. It forces hearers to encounter a message they might otherwise automatically shut out. We can use it powerfully to tell the truth, as Jesus did. We can use it to obscure the truth. We can use it to lie.

That's why we must think after we laugh. If the jest hides a dagger of truth and slips it between our ribs, we need to pay attention. If, on the other hand, the joke scatters seeds of deception on the soil of our hearts, we need to know that, too. Those seeds may soon be noxious weeds.

Telling the Truth

Humor can catch us off guard with the truth, but sometimes simply telling the truth can be funny. As Scott Adams of *Dilbert* fame observes, "You can make an ordinary situation funny by substituting honesty where, ordinarily, people would lie or avoid saying anything. Honesty in social situations is so rare that it automatically qualifies as bizarre."[1] The great humorist Will Rogers used to make the same point, perhaps too innocently, when he said he didn't create jokes but just reported what he read in the papers. We know they're both right, of course. Even though some papers and websites collect humorous "news of the weird" for us, we only need to read the ordinary news or look around us to see what's funny.

Humor can also reveal truth when it seems less obvious. It can open people's eyes to see things as they really are. Comic exaggeration, for example, can shine a spotlight on what should be obvious but isn't. It's like the young boy shouting, when the fashion-duped monarch was on parade, "the king has no clothes." Laying things side-by-side to show incongruity or absurdity can also make people laugh and see clearly all at once. Part of the power of this sort of exaggeration is that it may catch people off guard, prompting both laughter and insight.

Humorous truth-telling is practical and powerful, even revolutionary. Ernie Kovacs makes a practical point: "If you're going to tell 'em the truth, make 'em laugh, or they'll kill you."[2] But humor doesn't remove threat. That's why, from the beginning, political cartoonists have made leaders jumpy. That's why Hitler appointed special "joke courts" to keep people from naming their dogs and horses "Adolph." On the other hand, sometimes the powerful, in their self-absorption, don't see the threat. They don't get or even recognize the humor that will eventually undercut them.

---

[1] Scott Adams, *The Joy of Work* (New York: HarperCollins, 1998), 229.

[2] C.W. Metcalf and Roma Felible, *Lighten Up* (Reading, MA: Addison-Wesley Publishing, 1992), 187.

South Africa, while it continued its system of apartheid with all of its inequities and racism, provides one dramatic example of the power of humor in the face of fear. In the 1980s, during a period of stringently enforced censorship laws, comedy in theaters boldly undercut the status quo. Apartheid was not, of course, taken down by stand-up comics, but humor played a significant role. One of the most effective challenges came through the complex comedy *Woza Albert*, which was written by two black actors and staged by a white director. Through cartoonish depictions of characters, nonsensical dialogues, satirical mining of the nation's history, and much more, the play bombards white South African claims that apartheid was based on Christian principles. In its major plotline, Jesus returns to earth and goes to South Africa – much to the delight of its leaders. They brag to their critics that Christ "is back and South Africa has got him… . He chose us." When Christ confronts them for the oppression he sees, the leaders denounce him as a rabble-rouser and imprison him on Robben Island with Nelson Mandela and others sent there as rebels. When Jesus escapes the island by walking on water, two air force pilots first regret that, without their cameras, they've missed a photo opportunity – and then they destroy Christ and much of South Africa with an atom bomb. As comedy often does, *Woza Albert* ends with a scene of hope. Yet, throughout the play, apparently powerless characters in the story, as well as the play's audience, "use laughter as a weapon to ensure their survival."[3]

Another comic example from the same period is the character of Evita Bezuidenhout, a "fictional diplomat in drag." Created by Pieter Dirk Uys, Evita is on the one hand charming and apparently sincere, yet on the other a blatant racist who shows her views' absurdity with the ludicrous logic she uses to defend them. For example, in defending her commitment to reform she declares, "There are two things I can't stand about South Africa – apartheid and the blacks."[4]

---

[3] Ron Jenkins, *Subversive Laughter* (New York: The Free Press, 1994), 87-91.

[4] Jenkins, *Subversive Laughter*, 94-95.

Ron Jenkins' book, *Subversive Laughter*, engagingly reports on how humor helps effect social change around the world – from Bali to Lithuania, from Italy to Japan. Even if we hope that our jokes and story-telling don't start a revolution, it is clear that they can still effectively tell the truth.

Of course, the structure and devices of humor may, by design, involve trickery. They often involve misdirection and misleading set-ups, for example, to make way for surprise. Yet the substance of humor needs to be true. In teaching how to write comic sketches, John Vorhaus speaks of comedy as "truth and pain."[5] When we push mistaken thinking to absurdity or wildly exaggerate the contradictions of our lives, it should not only get a laugh but also reveal the truth. It may even challenge us to change our attitudes or behaviors in addition to recognizing the truth.

Sometimes we use humor to break down barriers between people so we can actually begin to listen to one another. Charlie Hill, a Native American from the Oneida tribe, uses humor to bring understanding and overcome ignorance. "I try to get people to hear a story they refused to hear before," he says. "I find when people are laughing, then we're connecting."[6] So also in speeches, in classrooms, in the banter of conversation, we often use humor not only to tell the truth but to help make truth-telling possible.

Humor not only helps people connect with one another, but it can also enable people to connect with the truth of their own lives. As we tell stories and make funny observations about our experiences, we invite people to see whether this is their story, too. Raymond Lesser recently caught me in this way with his article, "The Things I Can't Live Without." He begins, "My home is filled with the things I can't live without. I have spent my entire life carefully picking and gathering together these objects, so that now, in the full radiance of middle-age, I can

---

[5] John Vorhaus, *The Comic Toolbox* (Los Angeles: Silman-James, 1994), x.

[6] Joseph Boskin, *Rebellious Laughter* (Syracuse: Syracuse University, 1997), 175.

spend my spare time trying to create a clear path to move from one room to the next, without tripping and breaking my leg." He goes on to describe five categories of can't-live-without stuff, including "things I can't get rid of" and "things I wouldn't want to run out of."[7] As I read, I laughed, a bit nervously, and I was sure he had been taking notes in my garage (well, not just my garage).

Often cartoonists invite us to see ourselves in their quips and story lines – whether Peanuts or Kathy or Close to Home. John Callahan, a cartoonist I often enjoy, has a wonderful adaptation of "The Little Engine that Could" (the one that successfully climbed a steep hill while repeating, "I think I can. I think I can ..."). Callahan's "Low Self-Esteem Engine" stalls out while repeating, "I don't deserve to. I don't deserve to ..."[8] I've seen a lot of folks share a smile of recognition over that.

Sometimes humor can be tentative, just cracking the door open to truth-telling. Some subjects are simply hard to talk about, particularly with some people, and humor can often help open the way. That is why speakers often use humor to relax folks a bit and encourage listening. More directly, we can joke about how awkward it is to talk about it, since we share that. Or, when we disagree, we might be able to move toward productive conversation by chuckling together over the difficult issues and sticking points.

A student recently reminded me of how humor can help in establishing new friendships or in dating. Joking a bit can be a form of self-defense, a kind of hedge against rejection. With humor we can reveal little bits about ourselves to see if saying more about it would be okay. For example, you could joke or tease a little about liking snakes to test whether it would be okay to talk about the boa constrictor you keep in your car. Or you could joke that your car is actually a mobile herpetarium. In a

---

[7] Raymond Lesser, "The Things I Can't Live Without," *Funny Times* (April 2002), 23.
[8] John Callahan, *Digesting the Child Within* (New York: Quill, 1991), 12.

similar way, we can use humor to invite others to talk about something that might seem awkward. With humor we can offer acceptance and create space for getting better acquainted.

Actually, humor can sometimes be a first step toward confession. It may help us get the courage to say what we have to say about ourselves, even to ourselves or to God. I'm not suggesting at all that we should merely jest about or laugh off the truth about the core of who we are, whether it speaks of failures, successes, losses, growth, or whatever. But it's often hard to speak of deep things directly, and sometimes humor can help us speak of them at all. It can pave the way to speak of them with the candor, courage, and integrity that we need.

Obscuring the Truth

We often use humor to cloud things a bit, to make the truth less clear, or to soften it. Rather than being deceptive, we can jest in ways that show courtesy or kindness, that mark boundaries, or that simply divert or distract.

Especially in dealing with persons, we often do better to give the truth a gentle twist than to be brazenly direct. For example, euphemisms can often say what needs to be said, yet with a touch of kindness. In referring to social skills, I have seen understanding smiles show that the term "charm-free" has said enough. And personally, I much prefer the term "persistent," even spoken with a wry smile, to the word "stubborn." In music I've heard of people who always sing almost on pitch. We can choose to say "eager" rather than "pushy," "thrifty" rather than "stingy," "frustrating" rather than "infuriating." Often it's an even greater kindness not to mention it at all.

Humor can actually help tell folks not to mention it at all. It can warn, again in gentle ways, what not to talk about, what's off-limits. We often do this on the subjects of weight and age. Whenever my wife visited her mother, for example, my mother-in-law (may she rest in peace) would often ask her how much she weighed. My wife would always answer, "400 pounds."

Now this obvious lie (no, really!) was a way of telling the truth of limits: her weight was not going to be a topic of conversation. Similarly, we have a great variety of responses to questions about how old we are, from the eternal "39" to "old enough to know better." Funny replies to nosy questions often can help us move ahead in a friendly way.

Humor may also serve less directly to divert or distract from conversation about deep concerns, whether they be longings, losses, or anxieties. One could joke about the benefits of having lost a job. "It frees me to bring world peace." "I won't have to stay up nights worrying about how to spend all my money." As I write, I have a friend in transition who has a house to sell and a job to get. His half-jest, "It's just money," tries to maintain perspective and honor trust in God, but it also obscures a bit his genuine concern. It is a light way, it seems to me, of holding on to integrity. In right times and places we must deal directly with the challenges life brings. But sometimes, for ourselves and for others, diversionary truth-telling is exactly right.

Betraying the Truth

Just as we must see that humor is not merely frivolous, but can tell us the truth, we should also beware of the ways that it can deceive us. Comedy and cleverness in no way guarantee truthfulness. If we laugh carelessly we may well be hoodwinked or even allow the assault and undermining of cherished values. Certainly not every jest or laugh forces us to decide between enlightenment and perdition, but letting humor numb us can put us at risk.

We have seen how humor can be a tool to lighten or even defuse a situation and give perspective. We need to be careful, however, not to get carried away and fool ourselves. "Kidding ourselves" can become deceiving ourselves. This is a tricky question, though. As I've explored this idea, some people have asked whether we can actually use humor to hide the truth from ourselves. Somehow, don't we really know? Certainly we can use humor to distance us from the truth we know, to turn our backs on what we need to face, whether positive or negative. I sometimes have students, for example, who joke with me that they are slow or stupid, or that brain damage trashes any hope of success. I suppose some of them are right. But often I detect in the joking a fear of embracing the giftedness they suspect, or even know, they have. This isn't really self-deception.

Still I think we can, with or without humor, actually fool ourselves. We've all seen people use humor to trivialize or deny serious problems, whether regarding money, health, or relationships. The quip "denial is not just a river in Egypt" is well-known because denial occurs so often in experience. It routinely supports self-deception about addictive and self-destructive behaviors, and laughter empowers it all the more. Sometimes I hear, "I put off doing my big projects because the adrenaline rush of waiting until the last minute produces my best work." Or how about, "I can quit eating chocolate any time I want to. I just don't want to."

I've met individuals now and again who might be clinically classified as "jerks" but who seem entirely clueless about how steadily they offend others. When people respond coolly to their actions, they may use humor to deny they've acted rudely. Often enough the humor itself is rude behavior. "Hey, what's so bad about calling him a crash test dummy? At least I didn't tell him he's a couple fries short of a Happy Meal or that his cheese is slipping off his cracker – ha, ha."

We can also use humor to try to deceive others. A friend who is a wise listener reminded me, for example, of how people try to use humor as an eraser. Having said something too true or revealing, they have second thoughts and laugh. They hope the laughter or a little joke will persuade us that they were just kidding and will mask the truth that slipped through. My friend listens carefully to eraser laughter.

Joking to mislead is often more direct. We might use it to hide serious illness. "No, I'm doing great. I'll be chasing kangaroos tomorrow!" Hoping to escape being known, we may laugh away deep hurts, disappointments, and aspirations. "No, really! It only hurts when I don't laugh."

Advertising uses humor in particularly powerful ways. For one thing, since we're awash in ads, it needs to be very funny just to get and hold our attention. For another, as we should expect, it uses humor to slip around our defenses. Jean Kilbourne writes in *Deadly Persuasion,*

> The fact is that much of advertising's power comes from [the] belief that advertising does not affect us. The most effective kind of propaganda is that which is not recognized as propaganda. Because we think advertising is silly and trivial, we are less on guard, less critical, than we might otherwise be. It's all in fun, it's ridiculous. While we're laughing, sometimes sneering, the commercial does its work.[9]

In this sense, the apparent triviality of humor is itself deceptive.

The humor of the message itself may also deceive us. Of course we expect ads to stress the positive and neglect any downsides. But isn't it amazing how much fun and laughter goes along with almost any product? To that add lots of sex appeal and romance – often in a comical way. I really like the ones that promise that with the right car, jeans, or cologne, I will become delirious with joy and, finally, irresistible to others. We might expect great fun with a gourmet meal or a dashing sports car. But we're promised it, too, with underwear and suppositories and designer drugs we're told to ask a doctor about. Maybe that much laughter should warn us rather than take us in. After all, the fine print and fast talk on the ask-your-doctor ads usually admit you might get gastrointestinal debauch. The truth is, most of us have never had much fun with the runs.

Even if we laugh, we need to pay enough attention to correct false impressions, to resist false claims. Ads for beer give us a kegger full of examples. Such ads brim over with fun and funny. Frankly, I think they're often among the funniest and most

---

[9] Jean Kilbourne, *Deadly Persuasion: Why Women and Girls Must Fight the Addictive Power of Advertising* (New York: Free Press, 1999), 27.

clever ads running. Yet even with occasional feel-good, drink-responsibly spots, they scarcely give a clue about the enormous personal and social problems that alcohol causes. We would hardly expect advertisers to do that. Yet to keep perspective, we need to resist being taken in by the barrage of drink-up, have-a-blast deceptions. We need to remind ourselves of what we know about alcoholism, broken families, violent crimes, highway deaths and injuries, and much more that is directly caused by the use and misuse of alcohol. Ironically, though they worked hard to reduce the abuses everyone condemns, the historic Women's Christian Temperance Union has long been the butt of jokes in our culture, but you don't have to become an ax-wielding Carrie Nation to resist being shaped by funny fraud. Whether the pitch is for kegs, cars, or kitty litter, we can protect ourselves by naming and laughing at humor that lies.

In a similar way, sometimes we are fooled and fool ourselves by using humor to trivialize the serious and dangerous. We too easily want to "laugh off" our failures, risks, and destructive behaviors. We can even tell and deny the truth all at once. Taking the chance that you'll peg me as card-carrying WCTU, let's consider "drunk" jokes. They're funny and they're not. It's true that people act like fools when they're drunk, often in ways that contradict their normal behavior. They may slur their speech, exude beery boorishness, walk crookedly, even fall or pass out. In this we see absurdity, reversals, exaggeration – all the stuff of humor. And we may laugh about it with sympathy or even empathy, depending on our own habits of sobriety, I suppose.

Yet drunk jokes also fail to tell the truth when they portray drunkenness as insignificant. I'm sure that no one who laughs at such jokes really thinks that it's funny when DUI drivers kill themselves and others, when an inebriated student falls to his death from a dorm balcony, or when people have to put their lives back together after drunken date rape. Such events are common, as everyone knows, but to laugh at their cause masks that truth. Such laughter may even excuse ("yeah, but he was drunk, you know") or in some sense give permission for acting irresponsibly. I once had a friend tell me that he liked to drink a bit so that he could get rid of some of his inhibitions. In my case, at least, that instantly threw up red flags because I know full well that I need all the inhibitions I have.

Rather than binge on the dangers and deceits of alcohol, let's note that we may use trivializing humor to lie about many things. Sometimes we do it to fool others, or to collaborate in fooling each other, or simply to fool ourselves. It's a way of dealing with losses, embarrassment, destructive behaviors, and much more.

One place we all see trivializing humor is in television and movies. Situation comedies, for example, try to get laughs by exaggerating our conflicts, our pain, our stupidity, and our awkwardness in relationships. We often laugh when we sense that the sketch shares our experience; it captures truth and pain. We sometimes laugh in shock: "I can't believe he called her that!" As a practical matter of method, I think a lot of shows are so routinely rude that they don't surprise us anymore and just aren't funny, unless the meanness itself is what makes us laugh. But they do something else. They trivialize the harmful effects of rude, abusive language. Perhaps they even embolden us to think that's a good way to treat people to get a laugh. Similarly, comedy sketches sometimes present destructive behaviors as playful, innocent diversions. Sitcoms commonly treat lying, cheating, adultery, and other immoral behaviors in this way. Humorous stories of seduction and cuckolding are old and legion, but any alert person knows that such actions routinely wreck lives and families. At our best we know it's not funny – yet, if we don't pay attention, trivializing humor can weaken our moral sense.

Trivializing not only makes stupidity look good, it can also make goodness look stupid. Consider, for example, how often comedy presents principled people cartoonishly, as buffoons. People who see reality clearly and live in it with integrity are frequently played as moral aliens, priggish people who are completely clueless and who are trying to make sure nobody has any fun. Innocence is distorted to naiveté, kindness to gullibility. This kind of trivializing "makes fun" of the values that can bring us into lives of wholeness and joy. It deceives and endangers us.

The trivializations can be caustic, even cruel, but they may also be warm and apparently innocent. A thoughtful couple recently reminded me of the Tom Hanks movie *Big* as a good example. The movie charms and amuses in many ways as a prepubescent boy finds himself transformed overnight into a young adult. He soon becomes an unlikely marketing hero in the toy industry, innocently undermining company executives too full of themselves. He clumsily adjusts to being grown up. And, of course, he is drawn into a romantic, eventually sexually intimate, relationship by a beautiful young woman who can't resist his genuineness, his playfulness, his naiveté. In the end he returns to his childhood, his mom and dad, the guys in the neighborhood he bikes and plays ball with – but he has lost his innocence.

This astute couple noted at least two ways in which this fun movie trivializes the truth. First, they observed, if the lead character had been a young woman suddenly made a dozen years older, audiences would have been outraged at her treatment, especially in showing casual sexual dalliance as a warm, almost loving, gift. These viewers also observed that the movie scarcely hints at how costly and disruptive such a loss of innocence would in fact be. Even though I liked *Big*, I think they're right. Perhaps you will disagree about this particular example, but certainly these viewers demonstrate the kind of attentiveness that can keep us all from being easily taken in.

Resist! Rather than giggling passively on the couch, rise up. Be bold. Or lie there and be bold. We don't need to allow ourselves to be taken in. When humor abuses or deceives, don't laugh – or, if you've laughed, take it back. Laugh tracks mustn't program our sensibilities. I laugh a lot, but frankly there are plenty of things I don't laugh at anymore. We can actively reply to, even make fun of, deceptive humor. We can also choose not to watch programs or join in situations that routinely use humor to hurt or lie. We can resist and even rescue humor from those who corrupt it.

Surely we would enjoy living in an innocence where we could giggle or laugh without ever wanting to grab it back, where humor was really all in fun. But we know we can't. Still we need not abandon humor altogether, as some seem to do. Instead, as with any other good gift that gets abused, rather than rejecting it we can learn to use it with care and joy.

We can learn to use humor in ways that deepen our understanding and telling of the truth. We can learn to jest to mark limits and to show courtesy and kindness. We can learn not to fool ourselves or to be taken in through laughter. When we're attentive, even cautious, we can enjoy humor all the more.

6

Risks and Manners

As much as we enjoy humor, we also know it is risky. The devices of humor often require risk to be funny. When we exaggerate, push boundaries, or say the unexpected, for example, we tip-toe near the edge of a cliff. Sometimes, even in innocence, we fall off; sometimes people push us over. We've all been stung by a joke gone bad; many of us have watched our own words inadvertently sting others. Of course, a humor-free life has dangers of its own, so we're better off to manage the risks than to rid ourselves of them.

One approach to reducing risks is to acquire some manners, maybe compile a *Pocket Book of Humor Etiquette*. I don't quite mean "polite," though. That sounds too straight-jacketed to me, the stuff of snickers, little giggles, and starchy smiles. Wholesome humor sometimes puts its elbows on the table, slaps you on the back, and cackles a bit too loudly, though it will hardly go as far as to belch in someone's face. Manners at least recognize personal and social boundaries and avoid going too far.

Yet manners and safety tips to avoid falling off Humor Cliff seem merely defensive, even narrow. Wouldn't it give us books like *Games to Play in a Tux*, or *Jolly Pulpit Jokes*, or *Funny Stories that Won't Upset Grandma*. I'm not against clean humor. No, really! In fact, I find negative and smutty humor, so common now, boring – largely because it's so predictable, not to mention offensive. But simply avoiding bad words or offensive themes doesn't guarantee our humor will be positive or funny. I've heard "Christian" stand-up comics steer clear of bad words and forbidden topics yet still get laughs from negative, abusive material. The humor was sanitized, no doubt, but it denied a joyful spirituality. Even in performance comedy, surprise, absurdity, and other devices of humor have lots of funny territory to explore without being rude and offensive.

Instead of just trying to avoid offense, however, let's consider what would happen if our humor were to grow out of our dearest values. Surely it would help us live more fully integrated, consistent lives – a hallmark of spiritual maturity. It would also help us have more fun with humor.

What kind of values might shape our humor? How about adapting the Golden Rule: "laugh with others as you would have them laugh with you?" It's a practical way to think about generous love. Wouldn't that go a long way to assuring positive humor?

But let's go further still. Jesus said the commands to love God and love neighbor sum up the Law and the Prophets (and, of course, Jesus might be right about this). So let's look: what are the values we find here? Try these themes found frequently throughout the prophets: compassion and loyal love; justice and fairness; truthfulness and integrity; respect for others, taking particular care for the people who are often targets for abuse (widow, poor, orphan, resident alien); seeking wholeness (shalom); doing the right thing. As Jeremiah and his prophet buddies point out, God delights in these things (Jeremiah 9:23-24). We can even say they make God smile. So we're hardly surprised that Jesus likes them, too, and that he gives clear teaching about humility and servanthood. The fact my word processor doesn't know the word "servanthood" reminds me that many of these values are counter-cultural – but so is signing up for the Kingdom of God.

We don't have to imagine Jeremiah, armed with siren and whistle, leading the Humor Police and giving citations to humor scofflaws. These are not laws we try to avoid breaking, but a vision of life at its best that, in drawing near to and "knowing" God intimately, makes us smile and shapes our living.

Is this too high-minded for humor? I don't think so – particularly if it flows out of our natural spiritual development. People maturing in faith would naturally, if subconsciously, be asking themselves questions such as: Is this fair? Is it truthful? Is it kind? Does it unite or divide? As we grow in our Christian walk, and as we think more about how to use and enjoy humor in our day-to-day experiences and relationships, these values will more and more shape and inform our God-given sense of humor.

To press the point, let's think backwards. Do we really want to ignore integrating such central values at any point in our lives? Do we really want to say they're not relevant, to suspend them as if humor isn't part of real life? Do we want to act as if, when we're joking, being kind, fair, and truthful doesn't matter to others? Do we want to say that having these values interwoven into our whole lives doesn't matter to us? It's hard to answer yes to any of these questions. If we care about our core convictions, then we can't do just anything to get a laugh.

Values like compassion, fairness, integrity, and respect all share a common trait: they are practiced in relationship. Some folks think there is no genuine laughter that is not shared, though I'm not quite sure. I really enjoy being with myself and sometimes laugh out loud when I'm all alone. (Please don't tell my clinical psychology students, who worry about me enough already.) Still, most of our humor, certainly our most joyous humor, is shared. Which is why we must care for our relationships. They are the framework of our fun together.

C.W. Metcalf is particularly helpful in encouraging us to pay attention to our "audience," the people with whom we're sharing humor, whether it's an individual, a group, or a crowd. What are their needs, their experiences, their boundaries? In some settings we may also need to pay attention to an "accidental audience," people who may overhear and be affected by humor we share with friends. Metcalf offers this helpful rule: "If you pay attention to others' needs and feelings, you will rarely be guilty of letting bad timing turn positive into negative humor."[1]

---

[1] Metcalf and Felible, *Lighten Up*, 194.

Some Guiding Questions

We've been insisting that we can develop a sense of humor. In the same way, we can develop approaches to humor that reflect our values. Making good humor choices may seem awkward at times, but with practice they become habitual. We can identify some guiding principles and then practice them creatively as we grow.

The following questions suggest such principles. They are not rules as such, with the rigidity that might suggest, yet they help us reflect on our day-to-day experience and use of humor. Experimenting with them can lead us toward humor habits we can gladly own.

1. Is this a hit or a hug?

This is a simple test of love. Most of us know a verbal slapping around doesn't say love any better than a physical one. And most of us know the difference between an attack and an embrace. Hugs are better.

We see a lot of hitting with humor, of course, but the laugh comes from shock value, from our knowing how inappropriate it is. "I can't believe he said that!" It's over the edge. Consider, for example, this greeting a woman offered a not-close friend: "Well I see you're as fat as ever." Funny? No. Embarrassing and abusive. Sometimes you hear spouses beating each other in public over pet peeves in their home. He comments on how she burns some new dinner each evening or how she believes the Credit Card Fairy will pay for anything she buys with plastic. She may "joke" about his being a couch potato or an incompetent slob. Of course, all of this may be true and it must be judged in the context of both the relationship and the audience, but if such banter is fighting rather than playing, it is humor gone bad.

We can usually tell if we've crossed the line on humor, even if we're not getting punched in the nose. When we hear ourselves saying, "Just kidding!" or "What's the matter, can't you take a joke?" then we know we've gone too far. We're either trying to take it back, in a sense, or we're blaming the victim. Of course it's always better to avoid hurting folks, but when we discover that we have offended, we can take responsibility and make amends. That, too, encourages positive humor.

Christian Haggeseth suggests the following "humor affirmation." "I refuse to use my humor to express anger or prejudice; I will express negative feelings directly without contaminating my positive use of humor."[2] Addressing negative issues directly not only preserves positive humor, but also makes it more likely we can solve the problem.

Another temptation is beating up on people when they're not around. This still violates love, of course, but it also raises questions about our own trustworthiness. When we abuse others in humor when they're not around, people will rightly wonder whether we will do it to them as well. It puts our integrity at risk. Is love really a principle which permeates our living?

But there's more to hugs than avoiding hits. We've all seen the reminder, "Be kind – everyone you meet is carrying a heavy load." Humor laced with kindness can help lighten people's loads. Whether with friends or clerks or food servers, a warm smile and gentle playfulness can go a long way. Not long ago I made an afternoon run to the Coffee Cottage, my favorite coffee shop, where the young woman who waited on me seemed friendly, but burdened. When I ordered coffee and a "used brownie" (day-old goods), she laughed, then said, "That's the first laugh I've had all day." She needed it and was glad for it. Simple playfulness helped lift her spirits on a hard day.

2. Does this tear down or build up?

This question is rooted in respect. People of faith are to hold others in high regard, honoring them all as God's creatures, full of possibility and limitation. That's a given. Of course, individuals become unrespectable – scallawags, bigots, fools, crooks, jerks – which may cost them dearly in a variety of ways. Yet contrary to the natural impulse to dismiss and demean the rascals, we are

---

[2] Haggeseth, *A Laughing Place*, 142.

bound to respect their humanity still, to call to the God-given best in them and in everyone, to affirm and to build.

Insisting that humor respect persons swims against the current in a culture full of put-downs, "zingers," and "roasts" (a sort of ritualized celebration of insults and personal attack). Some is merely crude, some clever, some funny, some not. But it's very common.

Put-down humor first comes to full flower in the junior high years, as any veteran middle-school teacher or youth minister can attest. Kids are scrambling to work out an identity, to become an individual in some way distinct from the crowd, all the while coping with growth spurts, hormones, lots of chances for embarrassment, and zits. It's a tough assignment. One way to get through is to make yourself look good by making somebody else look bad. The put-down seems to be the perfect tool, even though it brings with it plenty of pain.

But it doesn't end there. We all know folks who haven't had a pimple in years who have never outgrown put-downs. There are differences. The insults may be cleverer now, and instead of just trying to find a place in the world, the put-down artist may be trying to secure a place as the Center of the Universe. It's not just play, it's a power play.

Admittedly, "zingers" can be fun. They can show creativity and playfulness. The serve-and-volley banter can be very witty and take surprising forms. Some classic exchanges still amuse us. One of my favorites is from Winston Churchill. Lady Astor, who was displeased with him, said angrily, "Mr. Churchill, if I were your wife, I'd poison your tea." Churchill quickly replied, "And if I were your husband, I'd drink it." Point. Set. Match. For all its high-stakes cleverness, this still is the kind of angry and hurtful exchange that does not serve relationships well.

Even though "can-you-top-this" banter can be fun, it can also quickly turn from playful collaboration to a fierce competition with an urgent need to best the other, to win, to have the last word, to hurl the zinger which leaves the opponent bloody and speechless. It may look like play, but it's not, as lingering hurts and doubts make clear.

It's not pretty to see colleagues tear each other down rather than build each other up. We have all seen competent people wound each other by dragging out zinger wars that should never have begun. How much better if we were simply to respect, and not try to best, one another.

"Roasts" share some of the same risks. "Friendly" fun easily turns fierce and, in my experience, the humor often quickly begins to carry bitter, angry messages not very subtly disguised. Certainly we can have fun with others, even put them at the center of attention, without shredding them. The devices of exaggeration and surprise, for example, can support playful meanderings through a person's strengths and passions. I once had the opportunity to introduce a good friend at an event where he was being honored for his notable achievement as a Christian leader. Of course, this provided a perfect moment for a roast and, given our history, he at least feigned being nervous about what I might say. Instead of needling him or spotlighting some flaw, I chose to exaggerate or focus on "hidden" or "secret contributions" he had made, depending on playfulness, absurdity, and laughter to hold him in loving regard before the audience. I noted, for example, that he served as a food service consultant for the Rocky Mountain Center for Fasting and Prayer and, with concern for bringing some gender balance to Christmas, was preparing a series of advent meditations on the Virgin Joseph. We don't have to be cruel to have fun.

The flip side of knock-down humor is humor that builds. As we noted earlier, humor can help us to cope, to survive, to grow, and to heal, particularly in the face of adversity. The ways we use humor with others can assist in that process. Through very simple humor we can recognize and affirm people's strengths, show our confidence and affection, and let people know we're glad they're around. Sometimes I'll ask student assistants in our office if they are in charge of the office today. When they say "yes," I'll act relieved and respond, "Oh, good, then I'm at peace." It's a way of showing appreciation and it's almost always good for at least a smile, usually a laugh.

3. Is this one-way or two-way?

We have the most fun with humor when we act as partners, when we play together in joking and laughing. Here's where give-and-take really pays off. Part of it is not knowing how the creative process will turn out. Part of it is permission we give each other just to have fun, to try to amuse each other. We use the phrase "give-and-take" to describe this process, though we sometimes use it negatively. That is, often we mean that one person can dish out insults but can't take them in return. (One way to check whether humor feels genuinely two-way is simply to ask, "Would this be funny if I were on the other side of it?") But the point here is that we have the most fun when we respond to each other. Putting aside how much I enjoy being with me, I love a good audience, and I need to be a good audience for others.

One of my wife's most endearing qualities is that she laughs at my attempts at humor, and groans. So do my children. Some folks think they shouldn't encourage me, but I think that's exactly what they should do – and what I should do for them. In being generous with our laughter, however pathetic the humor attempt, we nurture playfulness and collaboration.

In the context of deep friendships humor can flow freely and even break ordinary boundaries of appropriateness. One friend of mine enjoys a long-standing, cross-racial friendship in which racial humor flows freely. He and his friend call each other "nigger" and "honky" and tell each other shocking jokes to crack each other up. Two-way humor in warm friendship can, with some caution, cross those boundaries. This humor is used only between them, and not in front of others, who are sure to misunderstand. In the permission they grant each other, however, the brash boundary-breaking must be fun in itself. Beyond that, I imagine that it is a way of affirming their affection for one another and of parodying abusive ethnic humor itself.

Even outside such bonds, another way to encourage a two-way spirit in humor is to be slow to take offense. Some people can hardly wait for you to offend them, and if you miss them directly, they may get angry on someone else's behalf. It's better to give the benefit of the doubt. Until we know otherwise, when people offend, we can choose to assume they're not mean, but simply stupid.

4. Is this laughing at or laughing with?

One of Gary Larson's cartoons shows a pith-helmeted adventurer standing in front of a huge cape buffalo and working some sleight-of-hand with playing cards. His companion, standing at a safe distance, yells, "Goldberg, you idiot! Don't play tricks on those things – they can't distinguish between 'laughing with' and 'laughing at'!" Sometimes we don't either, though we should. There's a big difference between having fun and making fun.

In laughing at or making fun, we treat the targets of our laughter as objects, as things to be used for our entertainment. It's a one-way behavior that dismisses, at least in the moment, their dignity and our common humanity. It excludes them from our circle of humor.

I remember with embarrassment one source of laughter in my college dorm. One of the guys on the floor, let's call him Jerry, had a slight build, was not athletic, and was socially ill at ease. He soon became the object of dorm entertainment. The game was, when you saw Jerry coming innocently down the hall, to see how quickly you could take him down and pin him to the floor. The record was about two seconds flat. No contest, but always good for a laugh – a making-fun laugh that boosted the egos of his testosterone-driven dorm mates, hurt Jerry, and betrayed the values most of the guys professed. Even in dear friendships we need to be sensitive to boundaries and to apologize quickly if we offend.

5. Does this divide or unite?

This is a practical question for people whom Paul labeled "agents of reconciliation" and Jesus called "peacemakers."

Christians are called to break down walls, to invite people in and closer together, to help create *shalom* ("peace") as they seek wholeness, restored relationships, and community.

Comedian Danny Mora advises stand-up comics that this ability to gather people supports their effectiveness. In approaching an audience, he says, "It's not a combat or control issue: the challenge is to find what we have in common.... . When great comics succeed, they don't do it by fighting the audience. They do it by creating a community in time and space."[3] Certainly great humorists like Erma Bombeck, Bill Cosby, Garrison Keillor, and Rita Rudner excel in finding what we have in common. One of my friends always signs off his e-mail messages with "we're more alike than we are different." Unifying humor helps us explore that reality.

Milo Ross, the president of George Fox University during my student years, often brought people together with humor. Sometimes he would join students in the cafeteria line, a brave and comic move in itself, and heartily inquire, "And what kind of gastronomic debauch do we have here today?" When sharing a meal in a fine restaurant rather than the campus dining hall, he was likely to begin a sentence with, "Well, fellow sufferers ..." It's no wonder that such community-building humor endeared him to students.

Perhaps the question, "Is everyone having fun?" is a good test of whether the humor is unifying or not. If part of the group is being picked on or shut out, probably someone's not having fun. Even if they're not targets, people can sometimes be shut out and alienated by others who are having fun. For example, groups of friends or workmates who have strong camaraderie may tell "in-group" jokes in larger settings where their humor alone emphasizes that everybody else is not "in." Sometimes this is inadvertent; other times people joke with winks, nudges, and knowing smiles to make sure that outsiders know they're not worthy. In-group humor is wonderful, but it needs to stay in the group and not spill out to exclude others.

---

[3] Metcalf and Felible, *Lighten Up*, 189.

6. Does this tighten or lighten?

Depending on how we use it, humor can stand our hair on end and make us whisper "uh-oh" while we wait for impending doom. Or it can let the steam out of a pressure-packed situation. Humor can make people bristle or it can help them relax. One test of positive humor, then, is whether it releases tension or creates it.

An untimely quip or a tacky joke can supercharge a room instantly, regardless of its root – insensitivity to the audience, bad taste, or just ordinary stupidity. It could be blue humor at the PTA or a groom trying out mother-in-law jokes at the wedding reception. Regardless of its ill-fated origin, the moment is unmistakable – your lame attempt at humor makes people exchange worried glances and Dead Silence lands with a thud.

Some tension occurs naturally. It may grow out of trying to build relationships. It may occur in groups struggling to make a decision or perhaps even at loggerheads about what direction to take. A tasteful humorous remark or story well-timed can often open the way for continuing to work together productively. For example, when someone passionately overstates his point of view in a meeting, I've often seen tension relieved by the playful question, "Could you tell us how you really feel about that?"

To ask whether the humor tightens or lightens is to keep alert about permissions and limits. It's also a way of looking out for the vulnerable people who are easily hurt by bumbling jokes.

7. Does this blow smoke or shed light?

Positive humor improves communication. It brings understanding and opens the way to creative solutions. Without retracing our steps from Chapter 5 on humor and truth, let's note simply that positive humor is truthful. It clarifies; it shows reality; it reveals pain, absurdities, and possibilities. So if people not only get the joke but also get the truth behind the joke, we've succeeded. Or, looking from another angle, we may ask whether, in our use of humor, people can find us trustworthy, knowing that we've not used humor to distort, demean, or mis-lead. Being seen as a person of integrity in this way suggests that we may indeed be weaving our core values into our whole lives.

8. Is this costly or free?

Often humor is gloriously free. We can just play or be in fun and the laughs are free, no hidden charges. Quite literally, the more humor like this the merrier. But sometimes humor exacts a price and we need to ask, "Who's paying for this laugh?" I'm one of those people who, for a laugh, will happily pay the price myself. Self-deprecating humor and simply clowning or physical humor are ways of creating humor at your own expense, though I advise against paying an arm and a leg. Unless you're desperate. We may wonder, too, whether self-flagellation asks too high a price. You may be willing but you may also be sick.

Too often, I'd guess, it's someone else who pays the price – the target, the patsy, the butt of the joke. Here again we need to know our "audience." Sometimes targeting a person is fine in the context of a relationship based on mutual care and respect for each other's boundaries. As a guest speaker at our university, a friend used me as a humor foil, an easy target actually, to pry laughs out of the students. It worked well. After they laughed, a few students even feigned pity for me and asked later if I was okay. I was, because of our warm friendship and because he neither violated personal or public limits nor abused our mutual trust. We all had fun.

Being an unwilling target is quite different, of course. From experience we know it hurts, it seems unfair, it may open wounds and unwelcome questions. To be fair, probably only some of the people who create victims are evil perpetrators. Given the humor habits of our larger culture, it's easy to use other people to get a laugh. Yet using people contradicts the values that hold people in love and respect.

Knowing and regularly asking these eight reflective questions can help us shape sound humor habits. Such habits will guard our values and relationships and help us have more fun.

7

Humor at Home and Work

We are seeing how humor, in the context of our spiritual journey, affects our whole lives. We need, then, to pay particular attention to how we use and react to humor in the two places where we spend most of our time – at home and at work. How we use humor in both contexts is enormously powerful for good or for ill, so we need to think and act carefully.

Humor in the Family

When families practice positive humor, it brings many of the same humor benefits we can also experience individually. It makes our homes glad and inviting places. It creates perspective and reduces stress. As we share laughter, it draws us closer and frees us to reach our full potential. Many folks have experienced and witnessed just such homes.

Homes shaped by positive humor are exceptional, though I hope they are not rare. Yet often when I have spoken about this ideal, people come later to tell me wistfully, even sadly, that the families in which they grew up (or are still in) are nothing like this. One woman told me that in her family there was no humor at all. Another nearly cringed to report that the only humor in her family had been cruel and abusive, an experience that still makes it hard for her to enjoy humor. Still another person remembered that sarcasm was not only the main form of humor at home, but that it also was the only form of communication.

The bad news is that many families don't practice positive humor at all. The good news is that all families can laugh and enjoy it.

Of course, the dynamics of any family are bigger than humor. The ideal family is a place of love and mutual respect, a place to grow, gather strength, and come to our full powers. It's a place of nurture and mutual care. Sadly, not all families function this way, but we can scarcely settle for an "ideal" home in which we merely share a roof, store our clothes, and, on the run, tolerate one another as we wait our turn at the microwave.

If we don't pay attention, we tend to replicate the family experiences we've had. If these have been negative or somber or hostile to humor, change will require thoughtful attention. Even if we've had warm experiences, we'll need to be intentional to sustain positive humor at home. Short of conducting weekly "Let's Get Serious about Humor" seminars for the family, probably the two most effective tools for growing humor at home are creating a playful environment and modeling good humor practices.

Creating a playful environment helps us say we welcome and encourage humor. Rooms filled with treasures that make us smile or invite us to play can provide an easy start and steady undercurrent. In our house, family and guests alike enjoy glancing through the collections of cartoons or other fun books lying around. Current favorites include John McPherson's *Close to Home*, Gary Larson's *The Far Side*, and Scott Adam's *Dilbert*. Small games (that don't take a lot of time) and funny objects are tucked into nooks and crannies, not to mention the pleasantly goofy stuffed bears looking on from the edge of the family room. A winking, smirking Mona Lisa (a classic touch of sorts) crowns a bookcase filled with Mark Twain, Patrick McManus, Dave Barry, a collection of Pogo (in our house, Walt Kelly is unrivalled!), fun CDs and cassette recordings, and many more treasures. Foam-rubber noses, Groucho glasses, silly hats, and other simple costume paraphernalia sometimes hang out here and there. It's not messy or stuffy. I'm quite sure it violates Feng Shui (for the cosmically ordered household), but I know it's fun. Everyone's laugh-starter collection will be different, of course, but it helps when our homes themselves say, "Relax a bit, giggle, have some fun."

It also helps when we lighten up and try to keep perspective on what's important and what's not. We know that klutziness happens, even in the best of families, so when someone spills the milk we don't have to "have a cow." It could be – and will be – worse. Taking the big picture often tames a crisis. When we were struggling to potty-train our children, an older friend tried to help by reminding us they probably wouldn't be wearing diapers by the time they went to high school. (They weren't!) The prospect of long-term failure often brought comic relief in a frustrating moment. As we now share this wisdom with some younger friends, they sometimes laugh, too – depending on the mess and their level of sleep deprivation. Perspective-taking, even with humor, isn't always easy.

Lightening up can include keeping a patrol for Center-of-the-Universe behavior in ourselves and one another. After all, being self-proclaimed kings and queens who try to get their subjects to do their bidding can be no fun at all. We can forestall conflict more easily if we catch ourselves acting like royalty. Loretta LaRoche advises overcoming the temptation by exaggerating our sovereign presence – putting on a crown and cape, grabbing a scepter (keep these handy), strutting authoritatively, and laughing. It's the sort of confession others can receive. Offering a crown to other family members, however, may invite beheading or dungeon time. So might curtsies and scraping bows. Mimicry and sarcasm won't do in a situation that requires empathy, understanding, and creative response. We may sometimes need to be wily jesters to momentary kings and queens, though at other times we're smarter to heed the sign "Caution: Dangerous Despots."

Play Together

Simply playing together helps build an environment of family fun. That seems like a fairly basic concept, but families have to overcome a variety of challenges even to play together. Some families scatter so busily in separate directions they seldom enjoy each other. They may have to make time to play together or create rituals and celebrations that grow lightness and humor.

We need to consider, too, how we play together. Collaborative play often works better than activities which require "winners" and "losers." There's plenty of competition in the world and in families as it is. Making up a serial story, for example, in which each family member takes a turn telling a piece of the story, taps into the fun of creating and is usually good for laughs. Or we can clown for each other, tell jokes and riddles, read funny stories using "voices," play "hacky sack" or "Frisbee," share an outing, or even find ways to be playful in our tasks. We can regularly ask each other, "What did you do today that was fun?" And, of course, we can always be a good audience for each other, laughing generously at attempts at humor rather than competing or judging with responses like "well that's stupid" – even if it is.

Modeling humor surely does the most to sustain a fun environment and to teach good humor habits. It can start early. Infants and young children love to laugh, and the adults around them can enjoy and even encourage laughter. We need to use and invite humor that adapts to children's abilities as they grow and change, of course, but at all stages parents can set the example for joyful laughter.

As powerful as modeling is, ordinary experiences will also sometimes require direct teaching about positive humor. For example, this teaching may need to reinforce ideas of respect and boundaries. We may have to remind family members that calling someone a pimply-faced moron is not kind, funny, or wise, especially if you're talking to the king, uh, father of the household. We may need to remind family members not to "fight" with humor or to "laugh off" or trivialize serious concerns. We may need to interpret the humor of jokes or favorite family stories for children so they can share in these appropriately without being confused or misled. In doing all of this we may directly challenge the failures of humor in society at large. We will no doubt have to reinforce the difference between having fun and making fun. We may even teach ways to create positive fun and laughter.

Once the foundations are laid, the habits of humor and playfulness can animate family life in many ways. Humor can smooth making decisions together. Humor can inject playfulness into tasks and chores (which is not necessarily to say gladness or cheerfulness). A climate of humor can cushion the blows of the disappointments that inevitably come. It may even be able to take some of the sting out of moments of discipline. For example, one father I know, after explaining a disciplinary action to his daughter, was able to say, "You know that we're only doing this because we don't love you as much as the other children." It was so backwards that it prompted both a good laugh and a warm reminder of the deep love her parents did indeed have for her. Even when it's hard, firm and fun can go together.

An atmosphere of positive humor can also help soften and solve the conflicts that inevitably come in family life. We can use the creativity and perspective of humor to help us address puzzling problems. And, most of all, it can build a family's identity and togetherness. Laughter that grows out of a family's successes, failures, liabilities, and ordinary life lived joyfully together creates a strong bond. I felt this keenly with extended family as I laughed heartily with a cousin (of the "second" or "something-removed" kind) about the heavy burden our gifted family bears in knowing that we're almost never wrong. The confession and warning in our fun also brought us closer.

Much of this section has focused on traditional families, though many of these ideas can help those in different home and family circumstances. Pre- and post-children couples can create a playful environment, chuckle at (and forgive each other for)

klutziness, play together, and remember good humor principles. As empty-nesters, my wife and I are convinced that if you
share a living space with someone, you'd better laugh a lot. For
some folk, home and family may be a larger group of friends or a
church family. These ideas can work there, too. Finally, if you
live alone, please be playful and laugh at your own jokes. Certainly don't neglect other friendships, but you may discover
that you get a kick out of hanging out with yourself.

Humor at Work

Beyond the family, another place where humor can make a big
difference (and where we spend a lot of time) is at work outside
the home. The author of Ecclesiastes reminds us that work is
God's gift to us and that we should receive it gladly and enjoy it
(see 2:24-25; 3:22). Laughter can help us do so.

Many companies have discovered that humor can strengthen
the business environment. It can increase both creativity and
productivity. It can promote a positive climate in which good
working relationships can thrive. Humor can also improve
interactions with clients.

Some managers and businesses, understanding these
benefits, actively promote humor. Not surprisingly, some of the
companies regarded as among the best places to work have also
earned reputations for their humor. Among them are the ice
cream company Ben and Jerry's, Southwest Airlines, and the
British firm Virgin (trains, cola, and hot air balloon ventures
from its founder). Some set up humor rooms or humor carts,
both full of fun-inducing books, toys, recordings, and more.
Others appoint humor patrols (to see to it nobody gets too grim)
or mirth directors (to stir up good fun). Still others devise awards,
celebrations, and regular or even impromptu events to promote
humor. Robert Holden sums it up well when he talks of an
"I Care/You Matter/This Job Should Be Fun" management
style.[1]

---

[1] Robert Holden, *Laughter the Best Medicine* (London: Thorsons, 1993), 101.

Of course, some workplaces, like some homes, are a lot more fun than others. I worry about places where the CEO takes his cues from the leadership principles of Attila the Hun – though Attila may have been a scream (and I really don't want to offend any Huns). In an airport I once saw a young executive-type carrying a briefcase bearing the bumper sticker, "Have you flogged your crew today?" The message struck me as potentially humorous, but the guy with the briefcase didn't look fun at all. It may have been the whip in his hand and the clump of personal servants pampering him.

No doubt our workplaces differ widely, but regardless of management or the workplace climate, we can take humor to work in ways that energize us and our colleagues.

One of the easiest things to do is simply to amuse ourselves. We can practice taking ourselves lightly even as we take our work seriously. Chapter 2 suggested specific ways to do that, though we've hardly exhausted the possibilities. For example, C.W. Metcalf suggests wearing silly (not necessarily frilly, men) underwear beneath our look-how-important-I-am clothes, whether tailored suits or pinstripes. (Of course, this is just for one's own amusement. Metcalf makes lots of fun suggestions, some of which I'm too chicken to repeat here. Buy his book.) Looking at our high school yearbooks is sobering, but good for a laugh. "Self-defacing" humor can release tension and laughter at the same time. Simply take a photo of yourself and grease-pencil on sideburns, mustache, glasses, a gap tooth, a hat, or whatever you please. If you want, put it where you can see it now and again. As a way of befriending my mortality, I'm experimenting with making a temporary tattoo that reads "Certified Organic/ Biodegradable." Recyclable, too, even if you don't believe in reincarnation. Or, without schemes or props, we can just be a bit silly now and then.

Humor can also help us when we make perspective-taking moves on the job (or elsewhere). For example, Annette Goodheart teaches the value of describing our circumstances, however good or bad, and then adding "Tee-hee." "I got a raise – tee-hee." "They're sending me to Dull City – tee-hee." "Tee-hee" works better than you'd think.

Another perspective strategy is to sit loose and try not to take everything personally. Actually, humorous exaggeration can show us how silly it is to interpret actions and events as directed specifically at us. "The computer network went down just so I would miss my project deadline." "Who told all those people to call me just when I was finally getting some creative ideas?" Push "everyone's out to get me" to the heights! It's a great laugh – or, if it's not, it may provide a strong clue that you need therapy. At the very least we can follow Loretta LaRoche's advice, "Tolerate more, and give thanks often."[2]

We can also create a fun environment for ourselves. This can be very personal and unobtrusive, even for cubicle people. Did I mention my sequin-covered fairy godmother wand? I only use it once in a while to rescue the desperate, but just seeing it tucked away makes me smile. Entertaining cards, pictures, and sticky notes are in the mix, along with a "Smile-on-a-Stick," and a couple of miniature cars and an assortment of balloons tucked in a drawer. One author writes of keeping little toys in the pockets of all his jackets and another urges keeping a small humor box on file with a select group of stories, jokes, experiences, cartoons, and more that will make you laugh every time. Our personal choices will be quite different, certainly, but even in smaller ways we can all create an environment that amuses us and lifts our spirits.

A next step, again one more simple than courageous, is to share humor with our cow-orkers. Of course, all the principles of positive humor apply. We can hold each other in high regard and offer genuine gestures of friendliness, even if it's just a warm smile. Often with humor we can try to enter empathetically into the situations, challenges, joys, and sorrows of others. A person who has had a harried day almost always responds warmly to sympathetic humor. "Wow, you must have served a million people today!" In another setting, "It looks like all the really cranky clients especially chose you today," may have a similar effect. Or, having finally reached the front of a long line,

---

[2] Loretta LaRoche, *Relax – You May Only Have a Few Minutes Left* (New York: Villard, 1998), 41.

saying, "Been busy?" with a friendly smile can identify with a clerk's plight and prompt a smile in return. In the same way we can laugh with others about their successes; even small triumphs deserve exaggerated (but not mocking) praise.

Humor can also help us treat each other respectfully as humans, not merely as humanoids filling roles and doing jobs. Even small acts can make a difference. Recently I happened on our head painter while he was painting (again, of course) an art gallery wall. Noting the strong smell of paint, I said, "I wonder if you can get this fragrance in an aerosol can?" He quipped right back, "I don't know, but I have it in a cologne." In less than thirty seconds we shared a great laugh together and exchanged warm greetings. But that brief moment of playful conversation also reinforced our common humanity and mutual respect.

Another friend of mine, returning to work after lunch at a Chinese restaurant, unexpectedly asked his office partner, "Do you find me strangely mysterious?" After pausing to enjoy his friend's bewildered look and dismayed laughter, he continued, "The fortune in my fortune cookie said that someone finds me strangely mysterious, and I'm just trying to find out who it is." Belly laughs all around.

Spontaneity and playfulness can unfold quickly and naturally. I sometimes send notes on daily pages from an out-of-date Dilbert calendar or on funny sticky notes. A friendly note sent with a timely joke or cartoon works, too. A colleague in the math department thanked me and laughed again with me over a *Fox-Trot* cartoon I sent over that showed one of the characters golfing and yelling "$\sqrt{16}$." In *Managing to Have Fun* Weinstein advises people, "Vow to practice joy on the path to service."[3] Only an imagination infarction can keep us from finding ever fresh ways of practicing joy with humor.

Still another way to bring humor to work is to collaborate with others in creating a fun environment for everyone. Of course this works better if managers and supervisors encourage it. (Note to any sober-sided supervisors who might have

---

[3] Matt Weinstein, *Managing to Have Fun* (New York: Simon and Schuster, 1996), 23.

accidentally gotten this far in the book: Loosen up! Get with it!) Where managers are hesitant, they can often be persuaded by observing how the power of positive humor can not only create a climate of fun but can also respect the time, tasks, and practical needs of the workplace.

Shared humor need not be elaborate (though elaborate can be outrageously fun). It can be as simple as designating a joke wall or bulletin board to share humor. It could be the site for an ugly tie contest or a game of guessing who is who in baby pictures of employees. Another simple idea is to create little celebrations and reasons for them, maybe National Broccoli Day or a moment of silence to reflect on incontinence on continents around the world. Creating a calendar of celebrations can be fun in itself. Establishing fun rituals to welcome new employees or honor achievement builds a positive environment. Or you could hold regular "ceremonies" to give special awards, some funny, some in appreciation, some both. Even without establishing a "fun committee," which might be an oxymoron anyway, creative, joyful people can find all sorts of ways to bring humor into the workplace for everyone. The benefits are enormous and the possibilities endless.

Whether at home or at work, we can be ready to use humor to encourage, to brighten, and to show respect and love to those around us. We can also be ready, when people ask, to give reason for the joy that flows from our lives. They may be drawn to share it, too.

8

When It's Hard to Laugh

Sometimes it's flat-out hard to laugh, even when we want to. Though laughing might make more sense than anything else, though it might be good for us, though we might even know it's the best thing we could do, still somehow it's hard, even impossible.

We struggle to laugh for lots of reasons. Sometimes we're simply embarrassed, even over silly things. Sometimes pride will choke down laughter. After all, being the Center of the Universe is serious business. Sometimes stress, pain, or loss may get in the way. As one woman recalled, "I couldn't even laugh, I was in such a bad place." Another told me with sadness how humor had left her home for over a year while a family member endured treatments for cancer. We may need to be respectful and patient at times when humor seems to be no laughing matter. Still, we don't need to give in easily to the forces that would rob us of the lifting power of humor. Even when it's hard, we can learn when and how to laugh.

Embarrassment

Consider embarrassment, a simple yet annoyingly complex emotion. Adolescence brought plenty of embarrassment for most of us. I remember blushing and laughing at once when, after marching band practice, I split the back seam of my jeans in mixed company. I also remember sitting strategically in one place, still laughing with my friends, until my ride home arrived. Each day brings new opportunities for simple, seam-splitting embarrassment. We can wear mismatched shoes and socks, we can spill soup down our front, we can misplace our keys. In such cases of simple embarrassment, we're usually better off to laugh sooner than later.

But sometimes embarrassment is more enduring. We may fear we suffer from advanced stupidity ("well, duh … anybody knows better than that!"), like the thief at the glue factory who sniffed glue, passed out, and woke up glued to the floor where the police found him. It's easier for me, for example, to joke about split jeans than to laugh at my awkwardness – and fool-ishness – as a high-school freshman in offering a cut-glass heart pendant as a gift to a girl who had unknowingly won my heart. She was kind, I think, but clear. When I finally threw the pen-dant out some years later, embarrassment whispered to me again. I've never joked with others about this story or actually, until now, even told it. But I've found that recalling it with gentle laughter brings some freedom and understanding. Learning to laugh about things that make us blush, even if we never share them, can help us embrace our experience with more realism and grace.

Embarrassment can linger for a long time, due in part to a sense of humiliation or even high-stakes consequences. But learning to laugh about such moments can bring healing – and some great stories. I have a friend who, while dating his dearly beloved, was cited by a state patrolman for "driving while encumbered" (or was that "entangled"?). His buddies cracked up when he reported this to them in anger, but he stayed touchy about it for a long time. I haven't asked even now whether it's funny for him yet. But when I told this story in a workshop, one of the participants darted his hand up and, through his laughter, told us that thirty years before he had been cited for the same crime. I'm pretty sure that was the first time he'd told a crowd – and with such joy!

Tom Mullen tells a wonderful embarrassing-but-funny-later story about his participating as an honored student at Boy's

State in Indiana. Among the activities was a competition among the various dorm groups for the cleanest dorm each morning. Tom's group beat the other groups so badly on the first three days that the organizers of the conference recruited a retired colonel to give them the inspection of their lives on the last morning. They were ready; the room was immaculate. Failing to find fault with the room, the colonel walked down the line of young men standing at attention and stopped at Tom. Squinting at what could only have been the subtlest shadow of what might have been beard stubble, the colonel barked, "Son, don't you have a razor?" "Yes, sir," Tom quickly replied, "but I don't loan it to strangers." Apparently the colonel had never won a medal for humor. The dorm group flunked that inspection, lost the contest, and, to each young man, hated Tom. Tom could not even take credit for cleverness, I'm sure, since his reply had slipped past his lips before his brain noticed. He was devastated and, by his report, so embarrassed that he couldn't mention the incident, even to his family, for years. To share the story now, though, is to laugh until tears run down our faces. It reframes our experience in healthy ways and, for good or ill, it gives us a chance to lob humor grenades at our unnamed colonels.

Lest embarrassment cling to us for a long time, it's a good general policy to laugh quickly. When we lose our keys, for example, it can be really maddening and embarrassing until we find them, often in the perfectly sensible place we left them to keep them safe. Then, rather than berating ourselves, it's a good idea to laugh – not only in relief, but also admitting that the Klutz Factor still reaches us all. It might also be a good idea to include some self-deprecating humor as we apologize to those we've drafted or falsely accused during the search.

We may not come to laugh at our embarrassment just on our own. It often requires God's grace. Even when we don't know it, such laughter may come as God's gift to us. That's what my friend Virginia knew when, with moist and glad eyes, she told me how, after years of struggle, God had just that week helped her laugh about one of the most embarrassing and painful experiences of her life. Though her story's details are too painful and private to share here, I was moved to see how liberation and joy radiated through her thankfulness. No doubt there are times when this is exactly the grace we should seek. Grace is also needed when, instead of being embarrassed about what has happened to us or what we've done, we become embarrassed about who we are. This, of course, raises issues of shame that are beyond the scope of this book.

We can take practical steps that will enable us to smile at our embarrassment. One is simply to explore why we're embarrassed and then exaggerate. How big a deal is it? How can I make it bigger yet? Imagine clear to the limits how it could be worse. Play good news/bad news. The bad news is [name it]; the good news is [make something up or note something awful that didn't happen or something positive that happened in spite of it]. Or take a cue from Annette Goodheart – name the awful thing that happened and then add "tee-hee." Perhaps such playfulness can help break embarrassment's grip on us and renew our sense of joy.

Pride

Pride, on the other hand, undercuts humor much more deeply than simple embarrassment, even though they sometimes overlap. When pride blocks our sense of humor, laughing is more difficult and all the more necessary. Guaranteeing that others will find us important and respectable is grim work, after all – as is taking seriously the burden of running the world.

I don't think I understood that yet when my high-school vice-principal walked by and I whispered something to classmates about "Doc Anderson." Unfortunately he heard me and wheeled around with an angry correction: "That's 'Doctor Anderson' to you! I worked hard for that and you have to show respect." Sharply chastened, we stifled our laughter until he left the room, though the encounter did not deepen our respect. I knew nothing yet of the humorless things that can go with earning and wearing a doctorate. Now a veteran of academia, I've seen plenty of humorless, pretentious parading of credentials, of course, though I've also seen lots of wonderful humor – even among under-socialized, gifted colleagues.

Of course, we'll find vendors of grim everywhere. We'll meet supervisors and bosses who struggle too hard to be in charge and to make everyone know "we're serious here!" We'll see parents and teachers who urge people to "wipe that smile off your face." In such situations (and many others) joyous people can learn to fake and dodge. But when we're sobered by our own need to guard our respectability, to put our best foot forward, or to manage what others think of us, then we're at risk of terminal seriousness. Stifling our humor seldom reveals our best selves.

New college freshmen often face challenges of respectability like this. They are moving from the familiarity of home and friendships to new places, new people, and new expectations. Some have resolved to ratchet things up, to change who they are a bit, perhaps even to become more serious, more sophisticated. Many of them don't quite know when they can laugh, or even worse, when they can cut loose a bit to have fun, to share nonsense, even to join gladly in group silliness like C.W. Metcalf's "Howl for Joy" in which we howl at the moon in delight as we think of our favorite things. As most of us know, college freshmen aren't the only ones to grapple with ambivalence.

Learning the 18/40/60 rule could help us all. At 18 we're sure everybody's watching us and we care what they think. At 40 we learn not to care what they think. At 60 we finally learn they're not even watching. Maybe remembering the 18/40/60 rule can help us move out of the center of the universe and relax into being freer, more authentic and joyful.

Stress

Another enemy of laughter is stress. Stress! STRESS!! Stress can quickly stack up and weigh down our joy. Perhaps it's the whirling pace of the world and the choices we make or responsibilities that weigh too heavily. Maybe it's the assignment received today that was due yesterday or the need to accomplish more and more with less and less. Maybe it's the days even the dog snubs us. Or the snail mail, junk mail, e-mail, the spam in the hard drive or the peanut butter sandwich the children inserted in the DVD player. Maybe it's the stress that comes when we discover that everybody hates us for not having stress. When it doesn't drive people into maniacal cackling, stress often makes it hard to laugh.

As crazy as it seems, however, humor is one of our best antidotes to stress – as many books and studies have shown. It burbles up happy hormones to relieve stress. It helps reframe our perspective. It helps affirm who we are and gives us some feeling of power against external pressures. When performance demands wash over us, what could it hurt to say to ourselves, "And tomorrow after lunch we'll create world peace?" Exaggeration, absurdity, and other humor devices won't banish snarling stress, but they can help defang it.

Abraham Lincoln, as he led the United States during the Civil War, gives us one of the most telling examples of using humor to answer stress. Surely it was the cruelest of the nation's wars, and each day brought excruciating choices. Yet, much to the dismay of his advisors and friends, Lincoln often laughed. When they questioned him about this, he encouraged them to laugh as well and added, "With the fearful strain that is upon me day and night, if I did not laugh, I should die."

Losses

The losses we experience, whether great or small, can also make it hard to laugh. As we age, for example, many of us lose hair or 20/20 vision or our girlish figures. We may repeat ourselves or struggle with memory or repeat ourselves. Frankly it's not easy, though we have lots of humor about baldness, about bifocals and the length of our arms, and about, uh, forgetfulness. Some of our losses are annoying or embarrassing. (Recorded voice message: "Incontinence Hotline. Can you please hold?") Some point to larger realities, like they did when I tried to figure out what part of my trifocal lenses I had to look through to read the tiny volume numbers on my new hearing aids. (Then again, you don't want hearing aids big enough to display numbers you can read.) I could eventually deal with losing my girlish figure, but still the persistent little slaps by the ravages of time can both amuse and sober me.

Bill Cosby writes in *Time Flies*, "At my age, the hardest thing to do is accept what you are and not torture yourself with visions of what you used to be."[1] Of course, he knows, as we all do, that humor helps.

Sometimes our losses are sudden or grave. It may be serious illness, a painful family crisis, the death of a dear friend, or the loss of a job. Even here humor can help. It doesn't make the crisis disappear or take away the pain, but it does help us get through. Laughing doesn't trivialize loss, but it may deny its ultimacy.

When our eleven-year-old son got "juvenile diabetes" it changed his life and ours permanently, though laughing about awkwardness and mistakes in adjusting often helped in the process. When our friend Tom was diagnosed with juvenile diabetes in his thirties, he claimed to be developmentally "slow" and told pancreas jokes. Once at a camp I saw a woman who was completely bald sporting a shirt that read "Hair by Chemo." Her demeanor showed joy and courage without denying the seriousness of her challenge.

Our ability to laugh in crisis may help others endure as well. Prisoners of war, for example Viktor Frankl in Germany and Langdon Gilkey in Japan, tell how vital shared humor was in surviving their harsh treatment. The wonderful comedian Carol Burnett speaks of how humor helped as her daughter Carrie battled cancer. After having been released from the hospital, Carrie suddenly had to return. When her mom asked, "So you had to come back to the hospital, huh?" she replied, "I missed the food." The howl of laughter they shared drew them together and gave strength in a tragic moment.

---

[1] Bill Cosby, *Time Flies* (New York: Bantam Books, 1987), 123.

Many of us have shared laughter even at funerals. Indeed, telling humorous stories to express love and gratitude for the deceased is part of the tradition of the "wake." For people of faith, humor may even be heightened by the anticipation of eternal joy. I'll never forget, for example, the storm of laughter at the memorial service for my pastor Dave, who served in Christian circles where the words "dance" and "don't" always hung out together. When someone suggested that, though he had chafed at feeling he couldn't risk dancing here on earth, he was now dancing gladly in the streets of heaven, we roared. He would have shared our laughter, I'm sure, and in our great loss, we were comforted and buoyed by it.

Darkness

Beyond primarily personal crises and challenges, I find it hard to laugh when darkness seems to reign in the world, when oppression, injustice, and violence prevail, when the "wicked" and "fools" (to take up Old Testament terms) so easily succeed. It can be overwhelming and not offer much occasion for levity. Sometimes people who work hardest to bring light to the darkness have a hard time lightening up (though this is by no means a universal rule). Evil, after all, is not a trivial matter!

Yet even here we can take perspective and strengthen our hand by laughing. For one thing, even those who serve darkness fumble and bumble. It goes beyond stupid crooks. Just as really smart people do stupid things, so also really powerful people do stupid things, perhaps thinking that their power will shield them. Their actions and plans can be powerful and ridiculous all at once and give us reason to laugh.

At a personal level we can be alarmed and amused at the same time. We can laugh even as we resist. Or, even better, we can use humor as a tool of resistance. We can change the "spin" at times to point out that "the king has no clothes." We can set things side by side that clearly show how ridiculous certain policies and behaviors are and we can enjoy and support public voices who make such telling comparisons. For example, in addition to the power of political cartoonists and humorous commentators, which we've already noted, we can join the comic critique of music and film, including such classics as Charlie Chaplin's *The Great Dictator* and Peter Sellers' *Dr. Strangelove*.

We can also affirm and enjoy the larger picture. People of faith know at some deep level that God will ultimately get the best of it. People and actions contrary to God's purposes will be brought down. Psalm 2 portrays God laughing at those who rebel against God's purposes and God's "anointed one." The pretension of nations warring against "the Lord and his anointed one" is laughable, ridiculous on its face. Join in that laughter and be guided by its ultimacy.

Even in the face of darkness we can laugh now because God is sovereign now. The Bible is full of language and stories, often funny, about God taking down the proud and powerful (and raising up the weak and oppressed). It may be Pharaoh in Egypt or Babylon's Belshazzar at an imperial banquet where his knees knocked together and his legs gave way when he saw a hand writing on the wall. It may be Paul and Silas escaping from maximum security imprisonment or Jesus confounding Pilate with, "You would have no power over me unless it had been given you from above" (John 19:11). So God rules now; Jesus Christ has displayed and embarrassed vanquished powers in a victory parade – the most stunning comic reversal of all (Colossians 2:15).

The pompous and powerful only exercise power as God permits, even when we wonder why God sometimes permits. So we can and should always laugh at their sense of self-sufficiency. For nations and their leaders to take on themselves the name "superpower" or even "superduperpower" is flat-out laughable – not only because it's just silly to talk that way, but also because it is absurdly arrogant and self-assured. We can laugh, perhaps with sadness, because it is so out of touch with reality.

The Gospel of John tells us that in the hours just before those in power executed Jesus, he told his disciples, "Take courage [the old translations said "Be of good cheer!"]; I have conquered the world" (John 16:33). That victory's light pierces and overwhelms the darkness more each day and gives us reason for courage and "good cheer."

Sometimes it really is hard to laugh, even when we want to. After all, real suffering is often pervasive and prolonged. Yet we need to take the inability to laugh seriously, in ourselves and in others. To trivialize it or flippantly insist that people "just get over it" won't do. Still, we can learn to overcome barriers of embarrassment, pride, stress, loss, and darkness. We can learn to practice a habit of playfulness, to let a joyful undercurrent flow in us day to day. We can remember with tenderness the Klutz Factor, knowing we all have limits and we all sometimes exceed them.

Sometimes in a difficult time we'll say, "In five years we'll laugh about this." Another positive step is to ask what about the situation would make us laugh later and explore whether it might be okay to laugh even now. What's absurd or out of place or oddly proportioned just now that you could spotlight or exaggerate? If you could see it through the eyes of a friend with good humor instincts, would you see humor in it? No doubt there are times when it's too soon to laugh, but often it is possible and better for us to laugh sooner than later.

Ultimately laughter, even in hard circumstances, witnesses to God's power, love, and trustworthiness. Leslie Weatherhead once observed, "The opposite of joy is not sorrow. It is unbelief."[2] If we can laugh when pride betrays and stress frazzles us, when loss wounds and darkness overwhelms us, we are confessing that God is still in charge. Hallelujah!

---

[2] Leslie Weatherhead, *This is the Victory* (New York: Abingdon-Cokesbury Press, 1941), 171.

Part III
Enjoying God

9

Humor and the Old Testament

The Bible doesn't look funny. Often it's bound in black with bowling lane columns of fine print fenced in by cryptic cross-reference codes and explanatory notes. And a lot of what we read in the Bible isn't funny at all: boundary lists, genealogies, songs of pain and repentance, tragic stories of loss, even brutality, and much more – even though we may be perversely amused by threats of tumors and incurable itch.

Yet the Bible often is funny, just as we should expect it to be if it truly reflects the full range of faith and life. It includes, among other things, jokes and riddles, trickster and comic deliverance stories, humorous parables, even some "naughty" humor. And we don't have to be comic geniuses or Bible experts to get it. I'll suggest some clues for noticing the Bible's humor, and I'm guessing you'll be surprised at how much there actually is. In fact, we'll only be able to sample it, not give an exhaustive catalog.

Of course, there are folks who don't get it at all. Some make judgments about faith and Scripture that are simply bizarre. Consider, for example, this assessment from a professional psychologist:

> The Bible is a book full of tears but virtually devoid of laughs. Written probably by individuals who had rigid, punitive superegos, these writers did not possess ... the psychological *necessity for irreverence.*[1]

---

[1] Herbert S. Strean, *Jokes: Their Purpose and Meaning* (Northvale: Jason Aronson, 1994), 25.

I suppose it would seem rigid to tell him what to do with his superego, but he's missing a lot of good fun.

People of faith, otherwise very nice and thoughtful people, can also be humor-impaired. Perhaps they think that they are respecting the Bible by rejecting humor outright. Their familiarity with the Bible may blind them to its humor – or maybe they're just stiffened by frigid theology. They simply can't imagine or see anything funny in the Bible. Many of them are the same folk who stifle laughter in church. I hope they can all be healed.

Even people who agree that there is humor in the Bible may disagree about where it is. We have wildly different senses of humor, a fact often laughable in itself. Given this difficulty, you'll be glad to know that the International Board of Bible Humor has certified me as a "good but not foolproof guide" to laughing with the Bible. (The official guide patch looks a little goofy on my Bible cover, but I'm proud of it.)

Of course seeing humor in the Bible is not simply an exercise in frivolity. It influences our faith and understanding in several important ways – one of the most important being that, by including humor, the Bible points to a faith that engages our whole humanity, including our funny bone. Frankly, a humorless faith is not very inviting – not just as a matter of style, but because it fractures essential parts of our ordinary lives and tries to cram our bursts of joy into respectable containers.

While keeping an eye out for humor can help us enjoy the Bible all the more, more importantly, seeing its humor can help us better understand the Bible's intended message. Biblical writers used humor not just to engage readers, but also to reveal and emphasize truth, to make it stick. When we fail to see the humor we can actually end up with an obscured, even distorted, idea about what the writers wanted to convey. Jesus, for example, told his followers that they should gouge out their eyes and cut off their hands if these threatened their place in the kingdom of heaven. We can rightly relish both this saying's comic exaggeration and its serious point. But emergency room workers can often tell tales of patients who, understanding neither humor nor hyperbole, are eager to have offending body parts reattached. How much better if humor, not literalism, had kept them in stitches.

Actually I am urging a certain kind of literalism here; I believe we should understand the Bible as its authors intended it to be understood. So the point is not to take the Bible lightly, but to actually get the humor its writers used. In this search, it helps to distinguish between found humor and created humor. Found humor is when we discover humor the authors themselves intended. Created humor is when we introduce humor of our own as we read and reflect on the biblical text. One of the great examples of this is Bill Cosby's classic comedy routine about Noah. A lot of us have played with this text, too, wondering about termites or who had to shovel out the bottom of the boat. Both found humor and created humor are legitimate and fun, in my view, but, as with all biblical texts, we need to know the difference between what the Bible actually says and what we've added.

Clues to Bible Humor

Often people suppose that whatever humor is in the Bible is too subtle for ordinary readers to see. It's true, of course, that modern readers, who depend on translations, won't get wordplay humor in Hebrew or Greek, and they will probably miss humor that depends heavily on understanding an ancient culture. We'll miss a lot. Yet for all we may miss or may need help to see, there's plenty of humor that is perfectly obvious and nearly universal.

In trying to find an easy way to identify where the Bible uses humor, I have sometimes used the Cosby test: "If Bill Cosby were to read this text aloud, would it be funny?" This actually works, but it's imprecise; I've concluded that Bill Cosby could make even genealogies and instructions for sacrifices sound funny.

A more reliable path to recognizing humor in the Bible is simply to look for where the major humor devices of surprise, exaggeration, and incongruity (with their many variations) occur in the Bible. Sometimes I simply ask, "Wouldn't the folks in biblical times have enjoyed telling and hearing this story? Would they have laughed?"

Another helpful practice is to pay closer attention to the biblical text, including using our imaginations to enter into the text. The purpose here is not to invent scenes, but simply to visualize what the words describe. What would we understand if we were watching the scene instead of just hearing words? What would we see, for example, if we were to watch David trying on the armor of Saul, who is head and shoulders taller than the ordinary Israelite? Without stretching the text, I think we have physical comedy – a young lad clunking around in oversized armor. No wonder he preferred a slingshot (1 Samuel 17:38-40). Or what if we run a video in our heads of Elijah trash-talking the prophets of Baal on Mt. Carmel: "Maybe Baal's asleep … Maybe he's on a trip … Maybe he's, uh, watering the bushes!" (1 Kings 18). It brings the drama and humor alive. Words paint scenes, and we'll understand more if we see them.

In one workshop where I had announced the topic of humor in the Old Testament, one skeptical (and witty) participant also announced that it would be a short session. He had no idea about how I can stretch things out. He also had no idea about how much humor there actually is in the Bible. In the rest of this chapter we'll point to examples in the Old Testament, and in the next we'll explore humor in the New Testament, especially in the life and teaching of Jesus.

Sampling Old Testament Humor

A story very early in the Old Testament puts us on notice right away that we should expect humor in the Bible. It's as if this story has flashing neon signs or audience cue cards that scream at us, "Laugh! Come on, laugh, this is hysterical!" It is, of course, the story of Abraham and Sarah who have a baby boy named "He Laughs" (Isaac).

Ultimately it's a story about God's power, promise-keeping, and even divine preposterousness. But it's also a story about dashed hopes. They had once, long ago, had high hopes – and maybe a nursery. It's almost cruel irony for God to announce that, after decades of disappointment, after their chests have fallen into their drawers, they're going to have to turn the home office back into a nursery. Abraham and Sarah both cracked up at even the thought of having a baby now. Sarah said it best, "I can hardly remember menopause and he's even worse off" ("beyond Vigoro," she'd add, had she known). Maternity clothes always looked odd on her, as did the geriatric-plus waddle. The nine-month bulge and finally the bouncing baby boy made everyone hoot. Nothing, it turns out, was "too hard for God," and Abraham and Sarah laughed until they cried. No wonder they named him Isaac (Genesis 17; 18; 21).

Another type of humor we see in Genesis is trickster stories, most of them involving Jacob. For example, he used trickery to steal his older brother's inheritance; had a running best-shyster contest with his father-in-law Laban; and was cruelly deceived by his own sons over the disappearance of Joseph. From all the stories let's consider just two.

The first is the story of how Jacob tricks Isaac into giving him the death-bed blessing that is rightfully Esau's. It combines tragedy and comedy, which is not unusual in human experience. Isaac is nearly dead, his senses blunted – he can hardly see, smell, or hear – and Jacob takes advantage of this by pretending to be Esau. If we will, we can see him struggling to sound like Esau. Suspense and humor heighten when we see Jacob raise his goat-skin-covered arm for Isaac to touch and feel that this was Esau. We're told that Esau was a "hairy man," but goat skins? How hairy was this guy? The ruse works and Jacob has to run for his life, but we're left with both giggles and sadness (Genesis 27).

The second story is about Jacob on the run and taking a wife among his relatives in Paddan Aram. Smitten by the beautiful Rachel, Jacob promises her father that he will work for him seven years to marry her. When the great day finally arrives,

Laban pulls a wedding-night surprise by putting Rachel's sister, Leah (the one with the odd eyes), in all the wedding clothes and veils. By the time Jacob figures out that, just as his father blessed the wrong brother, he has bedded the wrong sister, it's too late. Like the blessing, the wedding can't be taken back and Jacob works another seven years for Rachel's hand – and its attachments (Genesis 29). Trickster themes laced with humor are quite common in the Old Testament.

The story of the prophet Balaam offers a hilarious but very different form of humor – a talking donkey. The donkey appears to be stubborn (of course!) when she is trying to save Balaam's life from the angel of the Lord whom she, and not the prophet-seer, can see. Already there are fun reversals. After Balaam has beat the stuffing out of the donkey, she turns and gives one of the most tear-jerking speeches you will ever hear: "What have I done to you? … Am I not your donkey, which you have always ridden, to this day? Have I been in the habit of doing this to you?" The angel scolds Balaam, too, telling him that if it weren't for his donkey's actions, the angel would have killed him and spared her (Numbers 22). She saved Balaam when he was ready to kill her.

The next two chapters about Balaam also include entertaining reversals. The king of Moab has hired Balaam to curse Israel. Three times the Moabites build altars and make sacrifices as a prelude to a powerful curse, and three times the only thing Balaam can do is bless Israel. Can you see a king hopping mad as his anti-Israel cursing system goes awry (Numbers 23-24)?

Another common humor device is improbable heroes who win with implausible schemes, and the Bible is full of them. Not all of them are humorous, I imagine, but many of them are. Several of Israel's "judges" clearly qualify. Gideon, for example, was hiding from the enemy, threshing wheat in a winepress, when God's messenger greeted him as "valiant warrior" (Judges 6:13). Gideon goes on to explain why he is the least likely to succeed as a deliverer of Israel.

The story of judge Ehud is rich with comic touches. His left-handedness makes him an unlikely candidate to deliver Israel from Moab. (How gauche! How sinister! Yes, we treat lefties a bit more nicely today.) He has a tricky scheme that includes a concealed weapon. His Moabite opponents are portrayed as fat (the king) and stupid (the king's attendants), another common humor device. Apparently Ehud kills the king in his private royal bathroom, locks the doors from the inside, and heroically exits through the only other opening.[2] He escapes while the attendants wonder how much longer they should allow the king to sit on the throne before they check to see if he's okay (Judges 3). Can we really imagine such a story being told with a straight face?

The stories about Samson (Judges 13 – 16) use humor as well, including his riddles, pranks, and his monumental weakness for short skirts and long eyelashes. However clever, strong, and even Spirit-empowered, he was also just stupid. The scene in Judges 16 is classic; we could get a laugh with this at any time in human history. Here's a script for the video in our heads: "Tell me why you're *so* strong." (He lies to her; she betrays him.) "Samson, you made a fool of me. Now tell me, really." (He lies; she betrays. Then still a third round.) Finally, "Samson, how can you say you love me and lie to me ..." Day after day she nagged, pleaded, batted her eyes at him, and played "if you really love me." Worn down, and a dim bulb at that, he gives in. In the end, of course, we learn that though Samson was not a stand-up comic, he could still bring down the house.

Even though the biblical writers use humor while pursuing their larger purpose, sometimes getting a laugh seems like the main point. For example, in one of the stories about David running from Saul (several of these include humor), David flees to Gath, one of the main cities of the Philistines, then Israel's enemies. When he arrived, some of the locals recognized him as their enemy's most successful general and, mistakenly, even called him "king." David's internal radar flashed warning signals, so he pretended to be crazy, clawing at the city gate and letting spittle run down his beard. He kept up his madman act

---

[2] Tom A. Jull, "MQRH in Judges 3," *Journal for the Study of the Old Testament* 81 (1998), 63–75.

even when they took him to King Achish. This sets up one of the great comic lines in the Old Testament. Achish scolds, "This man is insane! Why bring him to me? Am I so short of madmen here that you need to bring him here, too?" (1 Samuel 21:10-15).

Another of the funny Saul-and-David stories features one of Saul's ploys to get David killed by the Philistines. This particular story about Saul's strategy uses marginally "naughty" humor to great effect. When Saul sees that his daughter Michal has taken a fancy to David, he sends word to David that he'd be a fine son-in-law. When David replies that he's a nobody and can't afford a royal dowry, Saul makes a preposterous offer: you don't need money, just bring me one hundred Philistine foreskins. The Bible notes, perhaps unnecessarily, that Saul figured the Philistines would kill David before he completed his collection. After all, this is not like picking pockets where you can lift a guy's goods without him noticing. Still David thought this was a great offer so, with his troops, he sets off hunting foreskins. Next thing we know, David is back, eager to claim his bride, counting out two hundred foreskins in front of the king. ("One … two … three …" (1 Samuel 18:20-28).

The Old Testament is pretty earthy, so we need not be surprised at such humor. We see it earlier in a dark humor story about how Jacob's sons avenged their sister's rape. They agreed to overlook the matter if all the men of the offending prince's city would be circumcised. But three days after the circumcision ceremony, Jacob's sons killed them all, "while all of them were still in pain" (Genesis 34). The Apostle Paul angrily jests, I think, in his attack on the circumcisers bothering the Christians in Galatia: "I hope the knife slips" (Galatians 5:12, *Jerusalem Bible*).

To this point we have looked at humor only in stories, but we can find humor also in the prophets and other poetical portions of the Old Testament.

Let's consider first the story of the prophet Jonah, who is the comic opposite of your usual prophet. The story is filled with clever devices of reversal, exaggeration, and much more. When God calls him to go to Nineveh, Jonah boards a boat headed in the opposite direction. While a vicious storm terrifies the seasoned sailors, Jonah sleeps below deck. When they all are praying desperately to whatever gods they can think of, including Yahweh, Jonah, who as Yahweh's prophet should be an intercessor, never joins in. When Jonah eventually goes to Nineveh and makes a half-hearted attempt at preaching, the Ninevites (in Hebrew thought the worst people in the history of the universe) actually repent. And when their king finally hears of it, he makes the repentance official, including declaring a national fast and dressing everyone and everything in sackcloth, including Fido the dog and the cow old Bossy (not his wife).

God forgives them. And Jonah hates it. Instead of rejoicing, Jonah is furious and scolds God for being loving and merciful. "I knew you'd do that! That's why I didn't want to come here in the first place! So just kill me; I'm better off dead." In the end, God asking Jonah whether he shouldn't spare these people ("and also much cattle") brings the book to an abrupt, funny conclusion. The story emphasizes the unbelievably long reach of God's love, and the humorous telling makes it warmer and richer still. The preposterousness of the story in some sense mirrors the preposterousness of God's love.

Interpreters debate about whether the prophets themselves used humor. They cleverly used symbolic actions, songs, and all kinds of speech and literary forms to get their message across. So I believe they surely included humor and I am still exploring those great texts to identify where they did. Isaiah demonstrates what I mean.

The first example is a taunt song or satire against the king of Babylon in Isaiah 14. Not all satire is funny, of course, but I think this is. It belongs in large part to the popular category of takedown humor. The swaggering bully king who has brutally trampled kings and nations is going to get his come-uppance. This king, who had bragged that he would reach beyond the stars and make himself "like the Most High," is headed down to the world of the dead, and its residents are all astir to greet him. Their welcome includes phrases like, "so this is the hotshot king; now he's even weaker than we are … He's worse off than we are and won't even get a decent burial." And, in tribute to junior high humor, "maggots are spread out beneath you and worms cover you."

The second passage, from Isaiah 44:14-20, is also pointed satire, and I'm sure it passes the Cosby test. The absurdities beg for a laugh. The prophet pictures a man who takes a tree from his woodlot and uses some of it in the stove, some to bake bread, and some to cook burgers. But he also takes a chunk of it to his shop and, when he has carefully crafted it into an idol, he cries out to it in prayer, "Save me, for you are my god." Mr. Clueless doesn't have the wit, Isaiah notes, to say, "I've warmed and fed myself from this same tree. Am I going to bow down before a block of wood?" It's sad, and, in its absurdity, it's funny.

We might consider whether, even beyond their words, the prophets show humor. We've already noted Elijah's antics on Mt. Carmel. Elisha led a blinded enemy army into the heart of Israel's capital Samaria, and, instead of killing them, the Israelites put on a feast (2 Kings 6). Perhaps some of the prophets' acted messages amused people. For example, Ezekiel's months-long street theater surely provoked laughter as well as foreboding (Ezekiel 4). Perhaps dragging his luggage out through a hole in the wall did, too (Ezekiel 12).

The "wisdom" books also offer humor. We would expect that in Proverbs, given our general experience of adages, proverbs, and sayings. Humor is a device the sages often used to make the proverbs entertaining and memorable. Because Proverbs often uses wordplay and sound devices in Hebrew, however, we'll miss a lot of the clever humor. But there are still amusing images and characterizations (for example, the sustained caricature of "the fool"), "comic contrasts,"[3] absurdities, and good advice that makes you smile.

As a teenager I memorized this counsel that amused me: "And put a knife to thy throat, if thou be a man given to appetite" (Proverbs 23:2, KJV). Both the image and the quaint language made me laugh. Sometimes modern translations and paraphrases freshen and clarify the word pictures in Proverbs.

---

[3] Richard J. Clifford, *Proverbs* (Louisville: Westminster, 1999), 13.

Consider these two examples from Eugene Peterson's *The Message*:

> When you go out to dinner with an influential person,
> mind your manners:
> Don't gobble your food,
> don't talk with your mouth full.
> And don't stuff yourself;
> bridle your appetite. (Proverbs 23:1-3)

Or:

> A nagging spouse is like
> the drip, drip, drip of a leaky faucet;
> You can't turn it off,
> and you can't get away from it. (Proverbs 27:15)

Or note well this advice (from the New International Version) by letting it become a living scene in your mind:

> If a man loudly blesses his neighbor early in the morning,
> it will be taken as a curse. (Proverbs 27:14)

We can be open to the possibility of humor seasoning even the more somber wisdom books. For example, when I first read an article on humor in Ecclesiastes,[4] I was quite skeptical. However, I'm now convinced that if we abandon the deep gloom that we routinely impose on the text, flashes of humor do indeed show through. It may be in the reversals in chapter 10. Or it may be in the absurdities that the author points out: people working so hard to get rich that they don't have time to enjoy their money (Ecclesiastes 4:8–9) or who wind up leaving their fortunes to strangers and fools (Ecclesiastes 2:18-21; 6:2). Certainly Ecclesiastes isn't a comic essay, but it doesn't lack humor either.

Or what about Job? Am I stretching too far here, or is it okay to wonder, for example, if the exaggerated piling up of disasters and messengers of gloom tailgating each other may have a

---

[4] Etan Levine, "The Humor in Qoheleth," *Zeitschrift fur die Alttestamentliche Wissenschaft* 109, 71–83.

touch of humor? Or might we explore whether the bombastic rhetoric Job and his friends throw at each other might also provoke a smile? It's not the Three Stooges, to be sure, but it's not far-fetched to recognize that serious scenes sometimes effectively use humor. For that matter, even the grandeur of the "whirlwind speeches" (Job 38 – 41), in which Yahweh gives Job the pop-quiz from hell might make us smile, if nothing more than out of sympathy for Job's predicament or perhaps at how these speeches from God put Job's own grand self-defense speech (Job 29 – 31) in the shade.

We could look at still more texts, including the Apocrypha, to explore how we might see humor in the Old Testament, but I hope what we've done will encourage you to discover more on your own. My experience is that once we're open to the reality of biblical humor, new insights and possibilities pop up all the time. In the next chapter we'll use these principles in looking for humor in the New Testament as well.

10

Humor and the New Testament

"Jesus laughed." That verse ought to be in the Bible. Maybe the lost gospel industry will find it. Everyone who as a kid had to recite a memorized Bible verse knows its opposite, "Jesus wept (John 11:35)." He did weep, in this instance over the death of his friend Lazarus and later over Jerusalem. Jesus also suffered greatly during Passion Week, of course, as did his followers. Yet, even in this, he promised them that their grief would turn to joy (John 16:20), and Hebrews says that Jesus himself endured this suffering "for the joy set before him" (12:2).

Jesus as a "man of sorrows" is crucial to the Gospel story, but it's not the whole story. We are mistaken to apply that title to the rest of Jesus' ministry. His contemporaries certainly didn't. People crowded around him so thickly that he sometimes couldn't eat lunch. His detractors gossiped that he too often enjoyed the best parties in town, schmoozing with disreputable people. Even his first miracle, or "sign," according to John was to improve the beverage at a big wedding (John 2:1-11).

People loved to listen to him, too, and well they should. He told of good news for people who had had bad news as long as they could remember. He made hopelessly sick people well and sent them away grinning and laughing and praising God. And he loved kids. One of the things Jesus loved to do was welcome children when they flocked to him.

We have lots of paintings of Jesus, and most of them don't even hint that Jesus might be pleasant to be with. As Cal Samra points out in *The Joyful Christ*, through most of the history of the church, and even now, artists portray Jesus as sad, somber, morose, truly a "man of sorrows." Modern film portrayals often follow suit. In them we see Jesus as a gruff leader, barking at his disciples as they trudge over the hills, or as confused and wrestling with deep personal angst, or as distracted, gazing vacantly through laser-beam eyes. I suspect such images grow more out of the assumptions of the artists than out of the Gospels themselves.

What if we made a different set of assumptions? What if, without trivializing the significance of Jesus' mission, we assume that Jesus was, indeed, pleasant to hang out with? What if we were to see him as fun and sometimes funny? The modern musicals *Godspell* and *The Cotton Patch Gospel* both make this assumption and, where they do, I think they tap into the spirit of the Gospels. What else would we expect from someone who promised his followers an overflow of joy? Let's at least test the assumption that Jesus might actually have been fun by considering where we can see humor in his word pictures, stories, and encounters with friends and foes.

Look, for example, at some of the preposterous pictures Jesus paints. If we read visually we discover that Jesus' joke is, indeed, easy. Two such pictures come from Jesus' pestering the Pharisees about their obsession with the externals of religious purity. You scrub your cup and strain your drink to avoid swallowing so much as a gnat, he said, yet at the same time you gulp down a camel. To the playful image of a guy choking on a camel is added the irony that this hairy, humpy, much-more-than-a-mouthful overload was regarded as an "unclean" animal (Matthew 23:24; Leviticus 11:4). Jesus uses a similar visual joke, so to speak, when he needles the Pharisees for trying to get a speck out of someone else's eye while they have a log sticking out of their own (Matthew 7:3-4).

A camel's dumpy looks and odd manner (they're at least as funny as cows walking) suggest that camel humor must have been a hot item in Palestine. Certainly Jesus trades on it again when he warns that it's easier for a camel to go through the eye of a needle than for a rich man to enter the kingdom of God

(Matthew 19:24). Not getting the joke of threading a camel through a needle, interpreters have invented more sober explanations of this text, but Frederick Buechner captures the spirit of it in his paraphrase that getting a rich man into the kingdom of heaven is like getting a Mercedes through a revolving door.[1]

Earlier we commented on Jesus' teaching about throwing away body parts. Obviously Jesus meant business in this, but he used a wild and extreme image to get his point across. The high exaggeration is our main clue that it is funny, along with the fact that Jesus had no intention of founding the Church of the Maimed and Lame, always working short-handed (Matthew 5:29-30; 18:8-9).

Not only did Jesus use funny pictures, he also told funny stories. One of my favorites is about the king who forgave a servant's debt. The humor grows out of the story's exaggerations, reversals, and absurdities. It's sort of an Internal Revenue Service story (yeah, I know, *that's* not funny!) since the king was trying to get people to settle up with the government. One of his subjects owed millions of dollars and was about to have to sell his kids for it when he pleaded, "Be patient, I'll pay it all." The stupendous debt and his ludicrous promise combine for high exaggeration right away. But it gets better. After the king writes off this huge debt, the guy goes out and shakes down a friend who owes him five bucks, and, ignoring his friend's plea, "Be patient, I'll pay it all," has him thrown in jail. When the king hears of it, he drags the servant back in, angrily scolds him, and sends him off to jail "to be tortured until he should pay back all he owed" – translate: "life plus." Jesus sneaks up on his audience while they're still laughing: "This is how my heavenly Father will treat each of you unless you forgive your brother from your heart" (Matthew 18:23-35). Oh.

Jesus' stories, short and long, use a whole cast of comic characters who mirror our quirky humanity. Consider, for example, the crooked judge and the nagging widow (Luke 18:1-8), the neighbor leaning on the doorbell in the middle of the night and

---

[1] Frederick Buechner, *Telling the Truth* (New York: Harper & Row, 1977), 63.

the sleepy crank who bails him out anyway (Luke 11:5-8), the preening Pharisee and the desperately repentant tax collector (Luke 18:9-14). Or you could look at the dishonest manager trying to bail himself out (Luke 16:1-9) and that walking oxymoron, the Good Samaritan, not to mention the heartless "saints" who had gone before him, leaving the robbery victim to die (Luke 10:30-37). These exaggerated portrayals (and others) are really caricatures, and a clever teacher, which some folks think Jesus was, could surely play them at will for grins or belly laughs.

Even Jesus' teaching not based in stories may have shocked people into laughter. Luke 14 reports three of these during a Sabbath meal at a Pharisee's house. When they criticized him for healing a man on the Sabbath, Jesus responded with a teasing (and pointed) question, "If your son or your ox falls into a well on the Sabbath, wouldn't you pull him out right away?" The rhetorical question not only evokes a funny picture (so you're going to wait a day?) but also leaves his critics speechless, a funny touch noted by Luke.

Jesus next turns to ancient wisdom (compare Proverbs 25:6-7) about people who seat themselves at the head table and have to be asked to leave – a fun tweak of pretentious, Center-of-the-Universe types that we all know and love to laugh at. Finally, Jesus gives his host the most preposterous, upside-down guest list imaginable for his next party: forget your friends, family, and high falutin' types that are looking for their names and pictures on the social page and, instead, invite "the poor, the crippled, the lame, and the blind," the folk who never get invited to parties, even for campaign donations. This is an "equalitarian and inclusive" trait that often characterizes comedy.[2] To my way of thinking, that day Jesus limbered up an otherwise respectable dinner party.

Jesus shows his playfulness in encounters with both crowds and individuals. In the Sermon on the Mount, for example, he jests with parents as he points to the goodness of God. Eugene

---

[2] Conrad Hyers, *And God Created Laughter* (Louisville: Westminster John Knox, 1987), 75.

Peterson gets the spirit of it: "If your little boy asks for a serving of fish, do you scare him with a live snake on his plate? If your little girl asks for an egg, do you trick her with a spider? As bad as you are, you wouldn't think of such a thing – you're at least decent to your own children" (Luke 11:11-13a, *The Message*; compare Matthew 7:9-11). Even if we were to follow the traditional translation, "though you are evil," surely we have to see here that Jesus is talking with a grin and a wink, not a scold. He clearly credits them for being decent parents, setting them up to see God's loving care. Knowing that most parents worry that they're not good enough, Jesus' phrase "as bad as you are" (pause ... wait for the grins) points to God's generosity and, at the same time, teases a bit for a laugh.

Elton Trueblood suggests in *The Humor of Christ* that the puzzling story of Jesus' encounter with a Canaanite woman makes the most sense if we see banter in it.[3] Met at first with silence, the woman repeatedly calls on him to heal her daughter. When Jesus finally responds, he plays hard to get. His answer suggests she has only two chances, slim and none: "I was sent only to the lost sheep of Israel.... . It is not right to take the children's bread and toss it to their dogs." But she gets the best of the playful exchange: "Yes, Lord, but even the dogs eat the crumbs that fall from their master's table." Delighted, perhaps even chuckling at her clever response, Jesus commends her faith and heals her daughter (Matthew 15:21-28). Trueblood notes, "That Jesus was indulging in this kind of banter about racial and national differences is the only logical alternative to the insufferable hypothesis that He was being intentionally chauvinistic and rude."[4] It might well be that we would learn more, too, from Jesus' meeting with the Samaritan woman at Jacob's well if we were to hear more playfulness in their conversation (John 4:4-26).

The group Jesus has the most fun with is the Pharisees. Perhaps this sounds odd, because we know that members of the Pharisee Internal Security Squad were tailing Jesus constantly and, most of the time, were out to get him. I think we can assume

---

[3] Trueblood, *Humor of Christ*, 121-25.
[4] Trueblood, *Humor of Christ*, 123.

some of them were regulars and that Jesus probably got to know the unfriendly opposition by name. (Could this be roughly similar to the president's press secretary and the White House press corps?) If this is in fact the case, it only heightens the fun.

The "gotcha" game the Pharisees played, for example, certainly amuses us but also must have entertained Jesus' followers as well. The Pharisees would start the game with a trick question, trying to trap Jesus into doing or saying something that they could smear him with in the tabloids. But Jesus would outwit them, often set a trap of his own, and leave them looking like the religious Keystone Cops. With Zorro-like quickness, he deftly cut a "J" in their satin trousers while the crowds laughed in admiration. "Gotcha!"

"Tell us by what authority you are doing these things," they challenged him. Jesus offered to answer if they would answer his question: "Did John's baptism come from heaven or from men?" The trap was reversed and they finally pled ignorance (Matthew 21:23-27). Another time they flattered him shamelessly and then asked whether or not they should pay taxes to Caesar. Jesus noted their hypocrisy (the fawning speech was signal enough) and asked them to show him the coin they used to pay such taxes. As Doug Adams points out, this is already a "gotcha" because no self-respecting Pharisee would have such a coin with Caesar's picture and inscription on it.[5] But Jesus eludes and dazzles them even further with his answer, "Give to Caesar what is Caesar's and to God what is God's." They sneak away to change their trousers (Matthew 22:15-22). I'll bet there were some sly grins, too, when, one by one, the accusers of the adulterous woman slinked away to get out of their stone-throwing duds (John 8:3-11).

In addition to these and other "gotcha" stories, we also see places where Jesus hangs the Pharisees out to dry as the butt of the joke. I think Jesus was playful in doing this, but I'm sure the Pharisees didn't much like it. Some days they may have been after him as much for his humor as heresy. After all, Jesus'

---

[5] Douglas Adams, *The Prostitute in the Family Tree* (Louisville: Westminster John Knox, 1997), 7-10.

humor has an edge that cuts quickly to the truth. The jokes about swallowing a camel and having a beam in the eye are about them, of course, as is the quick-hit image of the blind leading the blind (Matthew 15:14). Probably my favorite is Jesus describing the Pharisee and the tax man at prayer. This passes the Cosby test hands down; it's read-out-loud funny just as it is, without adding words or details or anything else. A little vocal exaggeration and sense of timing can recreate exactly the devastatingly funny scene that Jesus intended (Luke 18:9-14). I'll bet that even some of the Pharisees who didn't have a mouthful of camel laughed, too, whether in self-recognition or in satisfaction because of how some of their strutting colleagues had embarrassed them.

To portray Jesus as a pleasant and funny person doesn't in any way cheapen his message or mission, nor does it even suggest that he was the sort of preacher who merely decorates the edges of the "serious" stuff with humor. Even when he was being playful or entertaining, Jesus used humor as one of his main tools to get his message across. Buechner even suggests that the parables "can be read as jokes about God in the sense that what they are essentially about is the outlandishness of God who does impossible things with impossible people, and … that the comedy of them is not just a device for making the truth that they contain go down easy but that the truth they contain can itself be thought of as comic."[6] The comedy of the gospel is about the preposterousness of God's love, the surprise of grace, and stunning reversals. It's about the Messiah mixing it up with sinners and IRS agents, outcasts and nobodies, the poor and the party people, who all turn out to be at the top of the guest list for the Great Banquet. The comedy of the gospel is about the extravagant, staggering, even scandalous deliverance that "fills our mouths with laughter." How could Jesus not use humor?

The Gospel writers, too, carry the spirit of humor in many of the incidents they report. Elton Trueblood offers a list of "thirty humorous passages" (including some of Jesus' teaching) in the

---

6 Buechner, *Telling the Truth*, 66.

Synoptic Gospels.[7] I may not agree with his judgment on each example, but I find others that he doesn't mention. In narratives, even short ones, there are glimpses of humor. Mark reports that, having arrived home at Capernaum, Jesus asked his disciples what they had been talking about while they traveled. Apparently the manner of the disciples' conversation roused observers' curiosity. "The silence was deafening – they had been arguing with one another over who among them was greatest" (Mark 9:34, *The Message*). Their embarrassment and the absurdity of their argument still strike us as comic. We get it (with a shared chuckle over the familiar Center-of-the-Universe behavior) even before Jesus makes the point more directly.

And there are fish stories. Who would enjoy a good fish story more than a fisherman? One tells about catching a fish with a coin in its mouth (Matthew 17:27). Another tells how, after getting skunked, the disciples caught so many fish when Jesus told them where to throw their nets that the nets began to break, and, even using two boats for the catch, the fish nearly sank them both (Luke 5:4-11). The last is another story of nets nearly bursting after a night of dismal failure. It's such a good fish story that we even have the count of the catch – 153 (John 21:1-14).

Others strike me as funny, but I'll mention them only briefly. The story of the short, rich tax man Zacchaeus works at several levels. It has a touch of short-guy humor, I'd guess, along with the image of the richest guy in town shinnying up a tree to see Jesus, and finally the great reversal of this despicable crook repenting and gladly giving away half of his wealth (Luke 19:1-10). The picture of Peter walking on water and suddenly sinking like a rock is great physical comedy (Matthew 14:25-33). When Jesus had 5,000-plus hungry people on his hands and the disciples were worrying about what to do, he gave them this instruction: "You give them something to eat." John notes that Jesus knew what he would do and said this to "test" them, but could it have teased them as well? It was obviously preposterous ("that would take eight months' salary!"), but it would have been fun to watch the disciples' head-scratching, sputtering, gasping,

---

[7] Trueblood, *Humor of Christ*, 127.

and stuttering objections to Jesus' first solution (Matthew 14; Mark 6; Luke 9; John 6).

The Gospels also report laughter that is not funny. Jesus is laughed at during his ministry and especially as he was bounced around between Pilate, Herod, and the soldiers for ridicule and torture. People jeered and laughed at him on the cross. Even the sign that Pilate posted, "King of the Jews," was a cruel joke of sorts. Peter, too, surely suffered taunting laughter once the folks around the fire had flushed him out as a Galilean and a friend of Jesus.

But in the end, when Jesus appeared among the disciples who were sharing reports of having seen him, how could there not have been laughter, the joy-from-the-heart-of-eternity kind of laughter? And when they all had a broiled, fresh-caught fish breakfast alongside the Sea of Galilee, how could there not have been wide grins and gales of laughter? It all seemed too good to be true, but it was true! The utterly impossible victory had overturned the darkest defeat they could ever have known. He is risen! He is risen, indeed! Yee-haw! Hoo-wee!

Luke and Paul Get It, Too

This great joy and high-spirited humor continues on beyond the Gospels. It's no surprise at all that Luke, who often included humor in the Gospel that bears his name, should also use humor when he wrote the book of Acts. Some of the humor is in pictures, some in story. One picture that never fails to amuse me is of the religious heavyweights, the Sanhedrin, completely confounded about what to do with a bunch of lay preachers taking over the Temple every day, accompanied by a well-known cripple who was now jumping up and down ecstatically and praising God (Acts 3 – 4).

One action they took was to throw Peter in jail. This set the young church to pack Mary's house full to pray "strenuously" for Peter's safety and deliverance. While they are praying, God breaks Peter out jail, in spite of the fact that he was heavily guarded, and he makes his way to the house. In Luke's own words: "When he knocked on the door to the courtyard, a young woman named Rhoda came to see who it was. But when she recognized his voice – Peter's voice! – she was so excited and eager to tell everyone Peter was there that she forgot to open the door and left him standing in the street." Luke reports further that the folks who had been praying argued with her that (in spite of their prayers) it couldn't be so. "You're crazy," they said. In the meantime, "Peter was standing out in the street, knocking away." Eventually they let him in and were nearly out of control (Acts 12, especially vv. 13-17, quotes from *The Message*). Is this a story that Luke or anyone else can deadpan?

Acts reports all sorts of amusing incidents. People who had been part of the whole kosher diet controversy surely got a kick out of Peter's vision of a shocking buffet loaded with ham sandwiches, cheeseburgers, and blood sausages (Acts 10). I smile at Paul and Barnabas trying to explain to the people at Lystra who are mobbing them that they are not the "gods come down" but really just humans. "No, folks, it's just Paul and Barnabas, not Hermes and Zeus. And don't have a parade and an animal sacrifice on our account" (Acts 14). Who could resist telling the story of the Jewish exorcists who, trying to imitate the apostles, get beaten up by an evil spirit and barely escaped naked and bloodied (Acts 19:11ff.)? And you can't leave out the story of young Eutychus who falls out of a third-story window, asleep, while Paul preaches (Acts 20:7-12).

Paul himself, sometimes maligned as humorless (among other things), shares in the humor in the New Testament. Frankly, that should not be surprising. After all, this is the man who wrote about the "foolishness" of the gospel and who, while in prison, wrote to his friends urging them repeatedly to rejoice (his letter to the Philippians). Paul uses a variety of humor techniques including exaggeration (both understatement and overstatement), parody, and a variety of funny images. We'll only explore a few examples here to further open our eyes in reading the New Testament.[8]

---

[8] Adams, *Prostitute*, Ch. 6.

An easy type of humor to identify in Paul is funny pictures. The best known, no doubt, is his writing about the body of Christ and how each member of it is important to the whole body. In high exaggeration he writes, "If the whole body were an eye ... or if the whole body were an ear" (1 Corinthians 12) – memorable and funny images. And with this he includes the absurd picture of the foot saying, "Since I'm not a hand, I don't belong to the body." Further still, he notes how the less honorable parts of the body are given special honor. The absurdity of these images brings smiles to his readers and strongly makes his point.

Even funnier is how Paul uses the idea of "foolishness" and being a "fool." The language of foolishness, folly, and fools has roots in the language of comedy – particularly as it relates to the gospel. The Good News stands the world on its head (surprise and reversal). It is preposterous, impossible, too good to be true. It is the unlikely rescue through the most unlikely means that fills our mouths with laughter. In the early chapters of 1 Corinthians Paul develops this theme in a variety of ways. He speaks of the foolishness of God! He writes of how God chose the foolish things of the world – the weak, the lowly, the despised – to shame the wise and strong, so that people would boast in the Lord and not in themselves. I imagine that he got a grin as he teased his audience that, when God got hold of them, they weren't much of a prize and neither was he: "Think of what you were when you were called." Of course, he soon turns from gentle jesting with these Corinthians to scolding them for their prideful fights and controversies.

He even turns the language of being the fool toward himself in a couple of extended passages (2 Corinthians 11 – 12) where he writes what Doug Adams calls an "antiautobiography," a parody of the self-serving autobiographies that were well known in the Mediterranean world at that time (and still are in our culture, for that matter). Here the exaggeration knows no bounds, and that's one of the cues that it's comedy rather than some sort of prideful apology for himself. Paul writes that he's been beaten over and again by the Jews and the Romans, shipwrecked three times, robbed, left for dead, thrown in jail, betrayed, hungry, naked, "at death's door time after time," and so on, "and that's not the half of it. I also have to take care of all these churches." I believe Paul uses such humor effectively to challenge his detractors who, in his absence, are trying to usurp his authority in a church he founded and loved.

The Corinthians had asked Paul about marriage, in particular whether they should marry, given the state of the world and their expectations of Christ's return. It sounds to me like Paul mixes some humor in his answer to them. He says that those who can't control themselves should marry (1 Corinthians 7:9). Later, though, he writes, "But those who marry will face many troubles in this life, and I want to spare you this" (7:28b). I know that when I quote that in a college classroom, it's good for a laugh every time. If Paul jests here, he also knows that in his time marriage could indeed increase the pain and difficulty of serving the gospel.

We shouldn't neglect, either, the gentle and loving humor that Paul uses with Philemon. We might say that Paul "humors" Philemon with praise, an exaggerated praise bordering on flattery, in order to persuade him to gently accept his runaway slave, Onesimus (whom Paul chose to deliver this letter). Friends know when they're being set up with such praise and expressions of love which, though genuine enough, are overdone. And they smile and laugh. They're glad for their friend and usually are glad to comply with the friend's request. The way Paul works him over here, we can be pretty sure that Paul and Philemon had enjoyed some good times together.

I've shared many examples of humor in the New Testament to show that it's not unusual. I've skipped a lot of examples because there's not enough room and so that you can continue to discover them for yourself. As with our reading of the Old Testament, part of the point is to help us all learn to understand the Bible more faithfully and to find even greater delight in reading it. Beyond that, I believe these reflections can help us grow in our vision of life's journey as disciples of Jesus. They help us see Jesus as a dear friend and guide with whom we may enjoy a life filled with joy and laughter.

11

Hilarity and Holiness

Becoming holy is more inviting than it's often cracked up to be. Even though God's words to us are clear enough, "Be holy, for I the Lord your God am holy," there are many misleading images that distort our understanding of what holiness means.

One such distortion portrays holiness as a kind of rule-keeping that looks more to externals than to inward realities. I grew up among Christians who (perhaps loosely) identified themselves as part of the "holiness movement" and who struggled with this tension. In those days some of these folk used markers in behavior and dress as evidence for holiness – modest clothes, no makeup, earrings, jewelry, lipstick – which did set them apart from ordinary society. For young men looking to date, this sometimes offered a kind of truth in advertising without misleading facial decoration, phony hair color, or fake body parts. In some cases genuine modesty could be quite smashing. At their best, of course, these folk knew that dutiful rule-keeping was not the heart of holiness.

I once saw praise heaped on a prominent Christian leader from another tradition because throughout a lifetime of public ministry he never laughed – apparently a mark of spiritual giants. This stunned me because, in my judgment, to be admired for being a perpetual sobersides borders on libel. I won't broadcast such slander by divulging famous Mr. Grim's name; his admirer may be wrong in this and in so many other ways. I remember laughing at things Mr. Grim said, though I don't think he intended me to. Still, in his defense, maybe Mr. Grim deadpanned jokes so subtle and clever that nobody, especially his devotees, ever got them.

Sadly, we too often think of "saints" as people who were constantly serious, brows furrowed in deep devotion. Ann Ball's fun book *The Saint's Guide to Joy that Never Fades* tries to counter that image with wonderful examples of joy in Francis of Assisi, Clare, and many others. Yet the fact of the book itself suggests that her numerous examples of joyful "saints" are exceptions to the rule (or to what many perceive as the rule). Yet God's "holy people" are full of joy and laughter. Doris Donnelly even suggests that a sense of humor is "a precondition to holiness." She continues, "A sense of humor helps the sanctification process because it encourages us not to take ourselves too seriously. Taking ourselves too seriously deals a lethal blow to holiness."[1]

If holiness is something more inviting than grim duty, then what is it? It's simply living gladly as the kind of people God lovingly intended us to be. It's delighting to know who we really are, restored in the "image of God" and relaxing into our partnership with God in embracing and renewing the world. It's trusting God steadily and craving God's teaching, letting it seep deep into our bones to guide us in living with responsive freedom. It is, as the old confession says, coming to know God and enjoy him forever.

Mirror, Mirror

How can humor help us live in this kind of holiness? One important way is that humor can be a mirror for our journey, helping us move toward congruence and integrity. In talking about knowing ourselves, A.W. Tozer says the last rule of self-discovery is what we laugh at. The humor we enjoy and create can give us some clues about our journey.

When we laugh at someone else's story about struggle and weakness, for example, we may feel suddenly caught: "Hey,

---

[1] Doris Donnelly, "Divine Folly: Being Religious and the Exercise of Humor," *Theology Today* 48.4 (1992), p. 392.

I do that! How did he know?" On a late-night show I once heard a guest host joke that it was hard for him to accept this appearance because he was so busy at home in front of the cable TV – watching the home shopping channels and scrambled porn. The audience erupted in laughter, partly in surprise and partly, it seemed, in embarrassed self-recognition. We may laugh at stories about people hiding evidence of their addictions – chocolate kisses, booze, office supplies. We may catch sight of our own reflections in the mirror when others joke about struggles in relationships and in the choices they make. We might catch ourselves not only laughing at a story about getting even, but also eagerly adding its method to our own arsenal.

Sometimes the mirror may make us look better than expected. Perhaps in an unguarded moment we'll discover we didn't laugh at ugly humor that we used to think was really funny. Or the mirror may reflect our use of sarcasm, insult, or ridicule in such a way that it will force us to consider what is in our hearts. Humor moves us toward holiness by helping us see ourselves honestly, for what we are.

Confession

After catching glimpses of ourselves, we grow by owning up to what we see. Confession is that acknowledgement, and humor can help us as we embrace our humanity with all its splendor and frailty. Humor doesn't need to trivialize confession or make it easy. It's hard to take responsibility for messing up without making excuses, without blaming others, without pointing out that others are bigger jerks than we are. It's hard to admit that we've been acting like the Center of the Universe and that we've wreaked havoc and wounded people in the process. Humor may help us speak of things that we might not otherwise be able to talk about at all. It may help us let go of defensiveness and begin to move toward authenticity, to relax in becoming our truest selves.

To add a note of caution, though, humor works differently in the varied forms of confession. Sometimes laughter can give us a way to own up, however awkwardly, to the ugly and stupid things we do. I might admit, for example, that when I resolved to live simply I bought three good books about it and went to two malls, three thrift stores, and ten yard sales to stock my wardrobe with simple clothes – and all this after I bought the necessary earth sandals. Or I might discover I've been so self-absorbed that I've been completely oblivious and insensitive to the people around me. I could play with humor to explore and mend my behavior. "How oblivious was I? I was so oblivious that … [fill in the blank]."

Humor can help warm the environment when we have to tell someone else about a way we've messed up. Recently my dad struggled, I thought, to tell me that in the process of caring for our houseplants, a kindness while my wife and I traveled, he had accidentally broken a little figurine of an angel. I quickly assured him it was okay, but I wondered later if it would have been easier for both of us had he started with a little humor. He might have said, for example, "While you were gone I killed an angel." I would have laughed heartily, but he may not have known that. For all he knew it might have been our indispensable and cherished Angel of Liminal Sanity.

The dilemma leads to a valuable distinction. Often we use the word "confession" to refer to apologizing or expressing regret to another. Using humor in this setting is possible, I think, but very tricky. The history of relationship between the persons involved and the tone of the remarks help define what's possible, but a few principles are clear. The apology must be unmistakably sincere. It must acknowledge the offense and take responsibility without qualification. Humor can be counterproductive in such a situation, since people could easily misunderstand humor as sarcastic or as trivializing the importance of what makes the apology necessary. When we're apologizing to people, we'll generally do better to leave humor aside. On the other hand, confessing to God might take several forms. Whether we speak in sincere jest or anguished lament, God reads and responds perfectly to what's really in our hearts. For example, it might help us to tell God in comic hyperbole about how rotten we've been. How about, "God, you know St. Paul and St. Francis aren't the worst of sinners like they claim. I am. Tell them to be quiet. I'm the sorriest sinner in the history of the cosmos." God knows how to sort out hyperbole, might even chuckle, but will certainly show compassion.

Perspective-taking

Beyond its value as a mirror and a tool of confession, another way humor helps us move toward holiness is in perspective-taking. Humor can be a tool in discernment. Coming to spiritual maturity includes learning the habits of listening, keen observation, and prayerful attentiveness. These help us to see reality whole as well as to see the contradictions, the absurdities, the ways the best in life gets thrown out of kilter. Humor is especially effective in identifying and revealing such distortions, and typically our best comics, from Twain and Thurber to Bombeck and Cosby, are those with the keenest insights into the human condition.

To restore perspective, humor can undercut exaggerations by pushing them to absurd extremes. This might free people who fall into "awfulizing" or "catastrophizing," declaring their circumstances or the world's to be the worst they've ever seen. Some people are constantly in this state. In fact, this unmatched crisis of hysteria threatens to bring down the world as we know it.

People can also distort in a more positive way. Years after he had first seen it, a friend of mine was still steamed at the misleading slogan posted by the First Church of the Happy Face near Tuskakeegee (note the giggling goodness in not revealing the church's real name). Their big billboard facing the highway read, "Cheer up! Jesus never had a bad day!" Most folk gasp and laugh at such blatant and damaging distortion. But for those who are deceived by it, such nonsense might be exposed by observing that Jesus on the cross didn't shout, "My God, my God, what a great party!"

Humor as discernment also reminds us of the difference between sin and stupidity, between klutziness and corruption. After all, a lot of failures and bad choices aren't really sin, but normal expressions of klutziness. They might include being a carnivore (or a vegetarian), dressing badly, or falling for lousy financial advice. On the other hand, some achievements over which we glow with pride may be sinful, from the Tower of Babel to the nuclear bomb. Sometimes humor can help us know the difference.

Humor can also help us sort out silly religious practices and acts of true devotion. One of my favorite "silly" practices is public prayer as an occasion for forgotten announcements and hospital roll call. "And Lord, we pray for Mabel who is in Good Samaritan Hospital, Room 342, recovering from having her stomach stapled. May she be well enough to attend the church's bean supper this Saturday evening at 7:00 p.m. in the Fellowship Hall." Surely we can all choose silly favorites of our own. Identifying them can help us come to know God more simply and joyfully.

Another way humor can lead us toward holiness is by giving us one more way to express love to others. Humor can extend grace, showing compassion and even offering forgiveness. It can say "I love you" and offer a warm embrace through its playfulness. The clowning of Patch Adams in the movie and in his real life does that, in my judgment.[2] Humor can offer encouragement, show appreciation, and affirm. Maybe one way of holding a friend in high regard is, during playful joking, to offer him a "straight line" on which to build a "punch."

The Little Flowers of St. Francis includes wonderful stories about Brother Juniper, a member of that first Franciscan community who was blessed with deep devotion, joy, and dangerous naiveté. The stories about Brother Juniper are told not only

---

[2] A book in which he describes his life and vision is: Patch Adams with Maureen Mylander, *Gesundheit!* (Rochester, VT: Healing Arts Press, 1998 [1993]).

with high hilarity at his antics, but also with deep love for him as a friend. For example, Juniper gave so generously to the poor that the brothers had to watch carefully lest he give away all their clothes, all the furnishings of worship and altar, or anything else at hand. Once, wanting to serve the brothers, Juniper offered to cook for them. According to their custom, he begged for and collected all sorts of food – chickens, eggs, vegetables, and more. To save precious time he decided to cook it all in a stew that would last two weeks. With great joy he dumped everything in the boiling stewpot – vegetables, eggs unshelled, chickens unplucked. The finished stew stunned the brothers, and their lack of enthusiasm dismayed Juniper, who was assigned other tasks from that time forward. We can still enjoy these tales, but surely the first brothers laughed uproariously as they told them with Juniper sitting among them. In joking about his naiveté, even silliness, the brothers also embraced Juniper and deeply admired his simple devotion to God.

Humor also helps deepen our growth in holiness by helping us hang on to hope. Sometimes the gap between what we long for and what we experience just hammers us. But humor can help us insist that darkness and defeat don't have the last word. To laugh when the shadows fall is not mere wistful whistling in the dark. It can affirm hope.

When the ancient Judeans were taken into exile in Babylon, they were devastated. "How can we sing the Lord's songs in a foreign land," they mourned (Psalm 137:4). Yet, according to some translations, they anticipated deliverance and the time when their mouths would be "filled with laughter" (Psalm 126:2). Part of hope is being able to laugh in confidence that light will overcome darkness and that the light at the end of the tunnel is not an oncoming locomotive.

One way to do that is to enjoy again stories of narrow escapes, of sudden reversals, of the hilarity of apparent weakness crushing the powers. It might be Daniel not sufficing as the snack *du jour* for hungry lions. It could be the Jewish damsel Judith carrying the besieging Greek general Holofernes' head from his tent in her handbag. In my tradition I chuckle to remember George

Fox preaching in a churchyard to a hostile crowd that grabbed a huge Bible from inside the church, rushed back out, and used it to beat him into bloody silence, heaped on the ground. What's fun is how Fox astonished them by standing again and, in God's power, continuing to preach. Or I think of Tony Campolo and his companions (he tells this story with great passion and laughter) who, exercising their right through holding only a few shares of stock, spoke to the board of a major corporation so powerfully that the board surprisingly acted with some justice and compassion toward poor folk in Haiti whom their decisions affected. Licking our chops in joy builds hope.

Besides celebrating past victories, we can also enjoy God among us now. And bold words then can guide us now. In 1663, the same George Fox wrote to Quakers harshly imprisoned (sometimes thousands of them, along with other religious Nonconformists): "Sing and rejoice, ye children of the Day, and of the Light, for the Lord is at work in this thick night of darkness that may be felt. And Truth doth flourish as the rose, and the lilies do grow among the thorns, and the plants a-top of the hills, and upon them the lambs do skip and play" (Epistle 227).[3] People of faith know that even in the most desperate times, God is present, God is at work. They know that, even though the victory may not meet our preferred timetable, God will prevail. Though evil and tragedy may victoriously strut by, we can chuckle as we anticipate their pratfall. With confident smiles we can look for the absurdities, the distortions, the cracks in darkness' armor. As in the *Wizard of Oz*, we can expect to find the little guy cowering behind the threatening curtain. Even in the face of death, we can rejoice and sing, "Where, O death, is your victory? Where, O death, is your sting?" (1 Corinthians 15:55).

As it moves us toward holiness, ultimately humor stands as a visible sign of faith and trust. It is a vehicle of joy as it helps us relax into God's care and purpose. This humor of joy has nothing to do with polite or nervous laughter while we sit on the edge of our seats hoping something good will happen. No, this

---

[3] Cecil W. Sharman (ed.), *No More but My Love: Letters of George Fox, Quaker* (London: Quaker Home Service, 1980), 76.

is relaxing deep into the cushions of the couch and letting unguarded toothy grins and belly laughs roll. After being weighed down and used hard, it's sinking into the reality of the rest Jesus promised, of the light burden and the easy yoke. It's relaxing into knowing we can fully trust God's power and loving intentions. It's knowing we don't have to be in charge or run the world for things to be okay. It's giving over our need to guarantee our own security. It's carefree delight in our life with God.

Jesus didn't actually give an Alfred E. Neuman speech: "What? Me worry?" But in the Sermon on the Mount and elsewhere he came close. "Why worry?" Jesus said. "It doesn't help. You can't use worry to add a single hour to your life or to change the color of as much as one hair on your head. Even at a dime a dozen God feeds the sparrows and knows when any one of them falls. God dresses the wildflowers to outshine Solomon wearing his best finery. And God cares more for you than for sparrows and lilies. God even knows every day how many hairs are on your head, as hard as that is. So don't worry. Relax. Keep your eyes on God and soak up the joy" (my paraphrase; compare Matthew 6 and Luke 12, for starters). This is what it's like to really know God and to "enjoy him forever."

An old English setting of Psalm 100 includes the phrase, "Him serve with mirth, his praise forthtell." Here humor as a visible sign of faith can become winsome witness. We not only trust and relish God's power and purpose, but we're glad to join in as light, salt, leaven, the aroma of Christ, as bright stars in the dark night. We may even gladly become "fools" for God in some sense, captured by the upside-down kingdom, by the "foolishness" of the gospel.

Who we are can make this Good News winsome as joy bursts through us. It can brim over and out of us because we're filled with joy as Jesus promised. No wonder Paul writes, even from jail, "Rejoice in the Lord always. I will say it again: Rejoice!" (Philippians 4:4). Right after that he tells his friends not to worry about a thing but to rely on God who is with them. Relax. Grin. Serve with mirth.

Perhaps humor is, as Doris Donnelly suggests, a spiritual gift, one to welcome and desire. But clearly humor is also a tool for any of us to express and deepen our life with God. It helps us see ourselves and then own up to what we see. It can give us perspective on what's going on around us. It can share love and hold out hope, and it can visibly show we are glad to know and enjoy God. And in doing this it moves us toward holiness.

Garrison Keillor reminds us, "Humor is not a trick, it's not jokes, it's not words. It's a presence in the world, like the presence of grace, and it's always there and shines on everybody." Let's welcome this grace and enjoy a life of holy hilarity. Let's create and share humor that lets our delight in God shine through. Let's laugh together in praise to God who is so eager to wash over us with rivers of joy and give us life to the full. Let's grin, giggle, and guffaw to the glory of God.

Questions and Activities

1 Humor Alert

1. Where do you most often encounter humor? Do you look for it or does it find you? Why do you think this is?
2. Describe your sense of humor. How did it come to be that way?
3. For you, what is almost always funny? Almost never funny? When is it easy for you to see humor? When is it hard?
4. What examples can you offer of "being in fun" rather than "being funny"?
5. In what ways have you observed that humor is good for you?
6. Recall a time when you embarrassed yourself by laughing before you thought. Why do you think you laughed? What did you do (or what do you wish you had done)?
7. Which theory of humor makes the most sense to you or appeals most to you? Why?
8. What is one way you'd like to develop or change your use of humor?

2 The Power to Laugh

1. How do you respond to seeing God as extravagantly joyous? If this idea seems strange or foreign to you, why do you think that is?

2. How much do you practice the habit of "being in fun"? What one or two practical steps could you take in order to "be in fun" more frequently and more wholeheartedly?
3. Could you find it funny to think that most people you see actually choose to dress the way they do?
4. What is one of your favorite ways of making humor?
5. What are some of the occasions when your creating something has made you grin or even laugh? How can you plan to enjoy your creative powers regularly?
6. Try to remember in your experience when laughter or playfulness has helped jumpstart creativity or solve a problem.

3 The Klutz Factor

1. What examples of death or near-death due to stupidity ("Darwin Awards" stuff) make you laugh? Which of them could have happened to you? What stupid things have you done that you were lucky to live through?
2. What types of Klutz Factor behaviors bother you most or are the funniest?
3. What is the klutziest thing you've done in the last month? Was it truly free of evil intent? (If you can't remember being klutzy in the last month, please schedule an appointment with your neurologist or psychotherapist.)
4. How does it make you feel to know that, as magnificent as you are, you have limits? And that it's God's idea?
5. How readily can you respond to your klutziness with laughter rather than anger or self-condemnation? What about to the klutziness of others?
6. What do you think of the suggestion that your response to klutziness may reveal your understanding of grace?
7. What practical steps can you imagine for moving toward a "humor of acceptance"?

4 Center of the Universe

1. How can you tell when someone is trying to become the Director of the Universe?
2. When are you most likely to act like King or Queen of the Universe? When are you most likely to expect people to use your royal title? What are some practical ways of recognizing yourself putting on your crown? Map out an escape route now to follow immediately when you next find yourself on the throne.
3. What are the best ways you can choose to appear cool and important, to convince people you are (or should be) the unrivalled Director?
4. What are the funniest (or most annoying) examples of oblivion that you have seen? If you've never noticed, can you explain why?
5. Without identifying the person(s) involved, what are the most fun examples you've seen about how vanity becomes laughable? (If an example is about yourself you can say so – but only if you can laugh about it now.)
6. Which of the ways of "stepping away from the Center" appeals most to you? What suggestions would you add that work for you?
7. When we try to move into the place where we can affirm that "it's not about me, it's about God," what kinds of confusion do we encounter? Is this tragic, funny, or both?

5 Sneaky Truth, Sneaky Lies

1. When we tell ourselves, mid-laugh, "Hey! That's not funny!" what kinds of things are we objecting to? Lousy humor? An attack on our values? A slap of truth that catches us off-guard? Or ...?
2. Give a few examples of when simply telling the truth can be funny. Can you give examples of how using humor can reveal the truth?

3. Why do you think some people in power get nervous about humor or even fail to recognize it?
4. Why is it important for humor to be "true"? What instances can you think of in which humor opened the way for truth-telling?
5. When have you seen humor used to "betray" the truth? In what circumstances do you feel most challenged by such deceit?
6. When or under what circumstances might you be tempted to use humor to fool yourself? To fool others?
7. What practical steps can we take to resist using or being taken in by deceptive humor? Which ones have worked for you?

6 Risks and Manners

1. Give a few examples of when, in using the devices of humor like exaggeration, surprise, etc., you got too close to (or even fell off) the edge of Humor Cliff?
2. How do you think observing "laugh with others as you would have them laugh with you" might shape your use of humor?
3. Think of a difficult or awkward occasion you have faced or might face. Suggest several specific ways you could use humor to make it easier.
4. Remember some times when you hurt rather than helped by using humor. What did you do to make amends? Which of them can you share with others now?
5. Which of the guiding questions gives you second thoughts about how you have used, or might choose to use, humor?
6. What other guidelines would you suggest that might help our use of humor be consistent with Christian living?

7 Humor at Home and Work

1. What are some of the ways you laugh or play at home? Which of them are spontaneous and which are planned? In what ways can you encourage an atmosphere of fun-filled spontaneity? In what ways can you plan for humor and fun?
2. If your family uses very little humor or destructive humor, consider why this may be so. What changes could make playfulness and humor more abundant and more positive?
3. Describe some of the fun experiences you've had at work. What helped them to happen?
4. List a dozen ways you might create humor for yourself at work (without bothering others).
5. What might amuse you, make you grin, play with your perspective? What are some practical ways you can bring positive, productive humor to your workplace? What can you do alone? For what do you need the help of others? Who might they be? How might you start?
6. Think of someone you work with during the work day. List several kind or playful things you might do or say to make him or her smile. Make such a list for each of the people with whom you work closely. Assuming that kindness or playfulness will not seem to you or them like a radical personality change, try some of your ideas. Plan and practice.

8 When It's Hard to Laugh

1. Think of a difficult situation in which laughter helped. Why did it help?
2. What embarrassments have you learned to laugh about and can share with others? Can you think of others about which it has helped to learn to laugh privately?
3. In which of your experiences has the ability to laugh seemed like an act of grace?
4. What practical steps can we take to avoid terminal seriousness?

5. What ways do you use humor to fight stress?
6. How can humor help us respond to loss? On what occasions has it helped you?
7. How is laughing in the face of darkness an act of faith?
8. Are there "in-five-years-we'll-laugh" places in your life where you can move up the schedule? Do you really have to leave the "I'll-never-laugh" places untouched?

9 Humor and the Old Testament

1. Does it surprise you to discover that the Bible uses humor? What in the Bible first made you laugh? Why?
2. How have you seen humor used effectively to communicate? In what ways do your observations help explain why a biblical writer or storyteller might use similar devices?
3. Why do you think some people (or perhaps even you yourself) hesitate to see humor in the Bible?
4. Why is it useful to distinguish between "found humor" and "created humor"? What guidelines can help us tell the difference?
5. Try reading (even aloud) some of the stories this chapter describes. Which of the biblical texts seemed funnier when you slowed down and tried to see what the words describe?
6. Why do you think the Bible might sometimes use "naughty" or even dark humor to help convey its message?
7. Besides the examples offered in this chapter, where have you laughed or wondered if you have seen humor in the Old Testament?

10 Humor and the New Testament

1. Start with Jesus. Imagine Jesus actually smiling at people, telling a funny story, teasing, joking, bantering, winking, waiting for a response. With this picture in mind, now read the Sermon on the Mount or some of the parables. (Maybe

read aloud to experiment with how to deliver a line.) How does this affect your understanding?

2. Which of the stories noted in this chapter seem funny to you? Can you think of some not mentioned here that seem funny? In each instance, do you think the laugh is found humor or created humor?

3. Which word pictures that Jesus paints seem particularly pointed and funny?

4. Who among Jesus' large cast of comic characters amuses you or even reminds you of someone you know?

5. How many pictures of Jesus that you know show him as happy or warm and friendly? How much do the common pictures of Jesus as sad or somber hinder us from seeing Jesus as joyful or even, at times, playful?

6. Sometimes hearing humor in Jesus' words makes them more powerful or even more understandable. What examples can you see of this?

7. How can humor help us understand the steady interplay between Jesus and the religious leaders?

8. What is humorous about the good news of the gospel? What can block people from seeing the comedy that's built right in? How does seeing the humor that's there deepen our understanding?

9. If Jesus was indeed joyful and used humor in announcing the Good News, we would expect his followers to catch on, too. What can we learn from how Luke, Paul, and others teach the truth?

11 Hilarity and Holiness

1. What aspects of teaching or thinking about serving God and being "holy" might lead people to think of holiness as excluding humor?

2. How can we use humor as a mirror of self-discovery? What have you discovered about yourself through humor?

3. What examples from your own experience illustrate how humor can help or hinder confession?
4. How can humor help us have a healthier perspective or grow in discernment?
5. How have you seen humor used to extend grace to others?
6. Why is it possible for humor to nurture hope? What examples can you give?
7. How can humor genuinely show our "carefree delight in our life with God"?

Select Bibliography

Adams, Douglas, *The Prostitute in the Family Tree* (Louisville: Westminster John Knox Press, 1997).

Adams, Scott, *The Joy of Work* (New York: HarperCollins, 1998).

Berger, Peter L., *Redeeming Laughter* (New York: Walter de Gruyter, 1997).

Boskin, Joseph, *Rebellious Laughter* (Syracuse: Syracuse University Press, 1997).

Buechner, Frederick, *Telling the Truth* (New York: Harper and Row, 1977).

Capps, Donald, *A Time to Laugh* (New York: Continuum, 2005).

Fahlman, Clyde, *Laughing Nine to Five* (Portland: Gilliland, 1997).

Goodheart, Annette, *Laughter Therapy* (Santa Barbara: Less Stress Press, 1994).

Haggeseth, Christian, *A Laughing Place* (n.p.: Berwick, 1988).

Hall, Doug, and David Wecker, *Jump Start Your Brain* (New York: Warner Books, 1995).

Holden, Robert, *Laughter the Best Medicine* (London: Thorsons, 1993).

Hyers, Conrad, *And God Created Laughter* (Atlanta: John Knox Press, 1987).

— *The Spirituality of Comedy* (New Brunswick, NJ: Transaction Publishers, 1996).

Jenkins, Ron, *Subversive Laughter* (New York: The Free Press, 1994).

Klein, Allen, *The Courage to Laugh* (New York: Jeremy P. Tarcher/ Putman, 1998).

LaRoche, Loretta, *Relax – You May Only Have a Few Minutes Left* (New York: Villard, 1998).

Lindvall, Terry, *The Comic World of C.S. Lewis* (Nashville: Thomas Nelson, 1996).

—*The Mother of All Laughter* (Nashville: Broadman & Holman, 2003).

Loomans, Diane, and Karen Kolberg, *The Laughing Classroom* (Tiburon: H.J. Kramer, 1993).

McGee-Cooper, Ann, *You Don't Have to Go Home From Work Exhausted!* (New York: Bantam, 1992).

McGhee, Paul E., *Health, Healing and the Amuse System* (Dubuque: Kendall/Hunt Publishing, 1999).

Metcalf, C.W.A., and Roma Felible, *Lighten Up: Survival Skills for People Under Pressure* (Reading: Perseus Books, 1993).

Mullen, Tom, *Laughing Out Loud and Other Religious Experiences* (Waco: Word Books, 1983).

Palmer, Earl F., *The Humor of Jesus* (Vancouver, B.C.: Regent College Publishing, 2001).

Radday, Yehuda T., and Athalya Brenner (eds.), *On Humour and the Comic in the Hebrew Bible* (Sheffield: Almond Press, 1990).

Samra, Cal, *The Joyful Christ* (New York: HarperCollins, 1985).

Trueblood, Elton, *The Humor of Christ* (New York: Harper & Row, 1964).

Von Oech, Roger, *A Whack on the Side of the Head* (New York: Warner, 1983).

Vorhaus, John, *The Comic Toolbox* (Los Angeles: Silman-James, 1994).

Weinstein, Matt, *Managing to Have Fun* (New York: Simon & Schuster, 1996).

Wooten, Patty, *Compassionate Laughter Jest for Your Health* (Salt Lake City: Commune-a-Key, 1996).

The author is a subscriber to *The Joyful Noiseletter*, founded in 1985 to provide pastors and church newsletter editors with clean jokes, anecdotes, and cartoons that can be used in their sermons and reproduced in their church publications and church web sites. *The Joyful Noiseletter* carries cartoons by 16 of the world's best Christian cartoonists. Annual subscription is currently $26 in the US and $36 in other countries. To subscribe or to order humor books, cartoon CD's, or prints, check their web site at: www.joyfulnoiseletter.com. Or mail to: *The Joyful Noiseletter*, P.O. Box 895, Portage, MI 49081-0895.